THE NATIONAL GLOBAL CHANGE RESEARCH PLAN 2012-2021

A STRATEGIC PLAN FOR THE U.S. GLOBAL CHANGE RESEARCH PROGRAM

About the National Science and Technology Council

The National Science and Technology Council (NSTC) is the principal means by which the Executive Branch coordinates science and technology policy across the diverse entities that make up the Federal research and development enterprise. A primary objective of the NSTC is establishing clear national goals for Federal science and technology investments. The NSTC prepares research and development strategies that are coordinated across Federal agencies to form investment packages aimed at accomplishing multiple national goals. The work of the NSTC is organized under five committees: Environment, Natural Resources and Sustainability; Homeland and National Security; Science, Technology, Engineering, and Math (STEM) Education; Science; and Technology. Each of these committees oversees subcommittees and working groups focused on different aspects of science and technology. More information is available at http://www.whitehouse.gov/ostp/nstc.

About the Office of Science and Technology Policy

The Office of Science and Technology Policy (OSTP) was established by the National Science and Technology Policy, Organization, and Priorities Act of 1976. OSTP's responsibilities include advising the President in policy formulation and budget development on questions in which science and technology are important elements; articulating the President's science and technology policy and programs; and fostering strong partnerships among Federal, state, and local governments, and the scientific communities in industry and academia. The Director of OSTP also serves as Assistant to the President for Science and Technology and manages the NSTC. More information is available at http://www.whitehouse.gov/ostp.

About the Subcommittee on Global Change Research

The purpose of the Subcommittee is to plan and coordinate the interagency U.S. Global Change Research Program (USGCRP), as described in the Global Change Research Act of 1990 (P.L. 101-606). The USGCRP provides for development and coordination of a comprehensive and integrated research program, which assists the Nation and the world to understand, assess, predict, and respond to human-induced and natural processes of global change. For more information, please visit http://www.globalchange.gov

About this Document

This report was developed by the Strategic Planning Integration and Writing Teams, which report to the Subcommittee on Global Change Research of the NSTC's Committee on the Environment, Natural Resources and Sustainability. The report is published by the National Coordination Office (NCO) for the USGCRP.

Copyright Information

NATIONAL SCIENCE AND TECHNOLOGY COUNCIL

Chair

John P. Holdren
Assistant to the President for Science and
Technology, Director, Office of Science and
Technology Policy

Staff

Pedro I. Espina
Executive Director

COMMITTEE ON THE ENVIRONMENT, NATURAL RESOURCES AND SUSTAINABILITY

Co-Chairs

Steve Fetter
Principal Assistant Director for
Environment
Office of Science and
Technology Policy
Executive Office of the
President

Paul Anastas
Assistant Administrator for
Research and Development
and Science Advisor
Environmental Protection
Agency

Jane Lubchenco
Under Secretary for Oceans and
Atmosphere and
Administrator of the National
Oceanic and Atmospheric
Administration
Department of Commerce

SUBCOMMITTEE ON GLOBAL CHANGE RESEARCH

Chair

Thomas Karl
Department of Commerce

Vice-Chair

Ann Bartuska
Department of Agriculture
Vice Chair, Adaptation Research

Vice-Chair

Mike Freilich
National Aeronautics and Space Administration
Vice Chair, Integrated Observations

Vice-Chair

Gerald Geernaert
Department of Energy
Vice Chair, Integrated Modeling

Vice-Chair

Timothy Killeen
National Science Foundation
Vice Chair, Strategic Planning

John Balbus
Department of Health and Human Services

Katharine Batten
U.S. Agency for International Development

Leonard Hirsch
Smithsonian Institution

William Hohenstein
Department of Agriculture

Jack Kaye
National Aeronautics and Space
Administration

Chester Koblinsky
Department of Commerce

Michael Kuperberg
Department of Energy

Linda Lawson
Department of Transportation

C. Andrew Miller
Environmental Protection Agency

Jonathan Pershing
Department of State

Joann Roskoski
National Science Foundation

Alan Thornhill
Department of the Interior

Linwood Vincent
Department of Defense

EXECUTIVE OFFICE AND OTHER LIAISONS

Steve Fetter
White House Office of Science
and Technology Policy

Thomas Armstrong
Executive Director, U.S. Global Change
Research Program, White House Office of Science
and Technology Policy

Katharine Jacobs
Director, National Climate Assessment,
White House Office of Science
and Technology Policy

Jason Bordoff
Associate Director for Climate Change
White House Council on Environmental Quality

Stuart Levenbach
Program Examiner
White House Office of Management and Budget

Fabien Laurier
Executive Secretary, Deputy Director,
U.S. Global Change Research Program

Strategic Planning Integration and Writing Teams

Craig Robinson, Chair (NSF)

John Balbus (NIH)
Shawn Carter (NPS)
Ralph Cantral (NOAA/NCA)
Nancy Cavallaro (USDA)
Randall Friedl (NASA)
Travis Haby (BLM)
David Halpern (NASA)

Leonard Hirsch (SI)
Jack Kaye (NASA)
Michelle Kelleher (NSF)
Kent Laborde (NOAA)
Fred Lipschultz (NASA/NCA)
Kit Muller (BLM)
Marilyn Suiter (NSF)

Michael Tanner (NOAA)
Rita Teutonico (NSF)
Chris Weaver (EPA)
Ming-Ying Wei (NASA)
Debra Willard (USGS)
Ashley Williamson (DOE)
Karen Wood (USGS)

National Coordination Office Contributors

Julie Morris, Strategic Planning Lead Coordinator

David Allen, Program Associate for International
Christa Blaisdell, Program Coordinator
Bryce Golden-Chen, Program Specialist
Jenna Jadin, Communications Coordinator

Alexa Jay, Program Specialist
Tanya Maslak, NCO Operations Manager
Aaron Smith, IT Manager
Emily Wasley, Program Associate for Adaptation

Advance Science Writing Team

David Halpern (NASA), Rita Teutonico (NSF), Chris Weaver (EPA) and Debra Willard (USGS) – Co-Leads
John Balbus (NIH), Anjuli Bamzai (NSF), Dan Barrie (NOAA), Bryan Bloomer (EPA), Jim Butler (NOAA), Nancy Cavallaro (USDA), Kelly Chance (SI), David Considine (NASA), Bert Drake (SI), Ben DeAngelo (EPA), Randy Dole (NOAA), Jared Entin (NASA), Nancy Grimm (NSF), Mohan Gupta (DOT), Renu Joseph (DOE), Erica Key (NSF), Dorothy Koch (DOE), Annarita Mariotti (NOAA), Dave McGinnis (NSF), C. Andrew Miller (EPA), Carolyn Olson (USDA), Rick Potts (SI), Richard Reynolds (USGS), Lucia Tsaoussi (NASA), Erika von Schneidemesser (NSF), Ashley Williamson (DOE)

Inform Decisions Writing Team

Randall Friedl (NASA) and Michael Tanner (NOAA) – Co-Leads
Denise Breitburg (SI), Joseph Bunnell (USGS), Sarah Burgess-Herbert (NASA), Thomas Cuddy (DOT), Anne Grambsch (EPA), Nancy Grimm (NSF), Jefferson Hall (SI), Randy Johnson (USDA), Mike Kuperberg (DOE), Jon Leland (NSF), George Luber (CDC), Meredith Muth (NOAA), Kim Penn (NOAA), Laura Petes (NOAA), Melissa Songer (SI), Jessica Tucker (HHS), Maria Uhle (NSF), Rose Wesson (NSF)

Conduct Sustained Assessments Writing Team

Ralph Cantral (NOAA/NCA), Travis Haby (BLM), Fred Lipschultz (NASA/NCA) and Kit Muller (BLM) – Co-Leads

Doug Austen (DOI), Peter Chipman (DOT), Ken Elowe (FWS), Malcolm Ko (NASA), Igor Krupnick (SI), Marjorie McGuirk (NOAA), Patrick Neale (SI), Paul Newman (NASA), Paul Schramm (CDC), Jonathan Thompson (SI), Luis Tupas (USDA), Bob Vallario (DOE)

Communicate and Educate Writing Team

Marilyn Suiter (NSF), Ming-Ying Wei (NASA) and Karen Wood (USGS) – Co-Leads

Celia Boddington (BLM), Michael Carlowicz (NASA), Caroline Crocoll (USDA), Nedra Darling (BIA), Cheryl Dybas (NSF), David Eisenhauer (BLM), Michael Greene (NASA), David Herring (NOAA), John Kress (SI), Michael Liffman (NOAA), Pete Marra (SI), Frank Niepold (NOAA), Jeffrey Olson (NPS), Brett Pelham (NSF), Rickey Petty (DOE), Jessica Robertson (USGS), Ansalan Stewart (NIH), Kimberly Thigpen Tart (NIH), Jermelina Tupas (USDA), Tara Weaver-Missick (USDA)

Technical Support

Banafsheh Azizi, Pat Corrigan, Rhonda Jackson, Ellen Kappel, Tala Karadsheh, Mara Sprain (NOAA), Stephanie Wade

April 2, 2012

Members of Congress:

I am pleased to transmit a copy of *The National Global Change Research Plan 2012-2021: A Strategic Plan for the U. S. Global Change Research Program (USGCRP)*. The USGCRP coordinates and integrates scientific research across thirteen agencies of the United States Government whose missions focus, to some degree, on changes in the global environment and their implications for society.

This plan was mandated by the Global Change Research Act of 1990 (GCRA, P.L. 101-606) and will serve as the guiding document for USGCRP for the next decade. It is built around four strategic goals: advance science, inform decisions, conduct sustained assessments, and communicate and educate.

In addition to these four goals, the Plan emphasizes the importance of national and international partnerships that leverage Federal investments and provide for the widest use of Program results. This Plan builds on the Program's strengths in integrated observations, modeling, and information services for science that serves societal needs and fully addresses the GCRA's mandate to "understand, assess, predict and respond to human-induced and natural causes of global change."

In accordance with the GCRA, the Plan was developed by a team of over 100 Federal scientists in collaboration with the USGCRP leadership. The team drew on the advice of the National Academies and feedback from public sessions with stakeholder groups.

The USGCRP is committed to building a knowledge base that informs human response to global change through coordinated and integrated Federal programs of research, education, communication and decision support. I look forward to working with the Congress in the continued development and implementation of this essential National program.

Sincerely,

John P. Holdren
Assistant to the President for Science and Technology, and
Director, Office of Science and Technology Policy

Table of Contents

List of Boxes

Executive Summary

The environment is changing rapidly. Increases in world population, accompanied by industrialization and other human activities, are altering the atmosphere, ocean, land, ice cover, ecosystems, and the distribution of species over the planet. Understanding these and other global changes, including climate change, is critical to our Nation's health and economic vitality. Scientific research is critical to gaining this understanding. Research, along with an array of increasingly sophisticated tools for collecting and analyzing data, can provide essential knowledge to governments, businesses, and communities as they plan for and respond to the myriad manifestations of global change, including sea-level rise and ocean acidification, heat waves and drought, and the severe storms, floods, and forest fires that pose an ever-growing risk to life, property, and agriculture.

To help fill this need, President Ronald Reagan created—and Congress in 1990 codified—the United States Global Change Research Program (USGCRP or Program), charged with providing a "comprehensive and integrated United States research program to assist the Nation and the world to understand, assess, predict, and respond to human-induced and natural processes of global change."[1] The Program coordinates the work of 13 agencies that fund research on global change, maximizing efforts and taking advantage of synergies while facilitating communication not only among member agencies but also with partners in industry, academia, and state, local, and foreign governments. Since USGCRP's inception, Federal research programs have created and maintained a robust mix of atmospheric, oceanic, and land- and space-based observing systems; gained new theoretical understanding of Earth-system processes; developed sophisticated predictive models; supported advances in data management and sharing; and helped develop an expert scientific workforce.

These research accomplishments have had far-reaching and significant impacts on the advancement and application of global change knowledge. For example, seasonal climate forecasts are now significantly more accurate and have longer lead times, often giving farmers critical and timely information for crop management. In addition, mathematical models of the general circulation of the atmosphere and ocean now can reproduce major features of the global temperature record of the 20th century, providing confidence that climate projections accurately reflect the link between rising levels of greenhouse gases in the atmosphere and planetary warming. These abilities are on display in a series of USGCRP publications that, over the years, have provided practical information about global change trends—in some cases sorted by geographic region and economic sector—to assist city and regional planners and others as they make decisions about upcoming investments in, for example, infrastructure and projected energy needs.

Today, new technological capacities and growing demands from a range of stakeholders for practical insights about global change require that USGCRP strengthen its role as both a generator and distributor of reliable, evidence-based climate change information. This Strategic Plan aims to facilitate this timely programmatic advancement. While the Program's first two decades focused largely on observations, process research, and modeling of the physical climate system, it is now poised to more fully integrate important dimensions to our understanding of the Earth system by incorporating such complex and critical components as the roles of ecosystems and human communities.

---

1. The Global Change Research Act of 1990 (Public Law 101-606)

This ten-year Strategic Plan—which reflects recommendations from multiple reports of the National Academies, dozens of listening sessions with stakeholders around the country, public comments on a draft plan, and collaborative planning among the USGCRP agencies—charts a course that will advance the Program's legislative mandate to deepen basic scientific understanding while providing information and tools to support the Nation's preparation for and response to global change. In particular, the Program will coordinate Federal research efforts through the following four strategic goals:

Goal 1. Advance Science: Advance scientific knowledge of the integrated natural and human components of the Earth system.

Goal 2. Inform Decisions: Provide the scientific basis to inform and enable timely decisions on adaptation and mitigation.

Goal 3. Conduct Sustained Assessments: Build sustained assessment capacity that improves the Nation's ability to understand, anticipate, and respond to global change impacts and vulnerabilities.

Goal 4. Communicate and Educate: Advance communications and education to broaden public understanding of global change and develop the scientific workforce of the future.

These four goals and their related objectives (**Box 1**) recognize that to respond effectively to global change will require a deep understanding of the integrated Earth system—an understanding that incorporates physical, chemical, biological, and behavioral information. Looking forward, USGCRP will accomplish this by supporting the use of advanced computing science and analytic technologies capable of spanning traditional scientific disciplines and also integrating research findings from the ecological, social, and economic sciences, with ongoing coordinated emphases on observations and modeling.

In furtherance of its mission to inform decision makers with the best global change-related information available, USGCRP is also committed under its new Strategic Plan to improving its assessment—and ensuring its fulfillment—of stakeholder needs. Farmers, as previously noted, depend on USGCRP-generated information to manage planting decisions as growing zones, pest and weed ranges, and seasonal boundaries shift. Health care providers need predictive models to prepare for anticipated increases in severe weather events and outbreaks of diseases previously uncommon in their regions. Insurers must account for the increased likelihood of weather extremes as they assess future financial risk. Inhabitants of coastal cities need to understand the implications of sea-level rise, especially in the context of novel storm patterns and other pending changes. Water resources, energy, and infrastructure planners need to address accelerating changes in the availability of freshwater, demands for energy, and needs to divert stormwater runoff. By considering and responding to these societal needs, the Program will not only enhance its immediate value to the Nation but also improve its ability to make wise decisions about future research directions.

Providing decision makers with timely and relevant information requires regular evaluations and assessments. As part of its mandate to perform periodic assessments, USGCRP will implement a long-term, consistent, and ongoing process for evaluating global change risks and opportunities across diverse regions and sectors. Specifically, rather than conducting such assessments periodically, as was the case during the Program's first decades, USGCRP will work to establish a sustained assessment capacity focused on evaluating the state of scientific knowledge related to impacts and trends, and on informing the Nation's activities in adaptation and mitigation.

But to be fully effective, USGCRP must communicate with more than just decision makers; engagement with the public is also essential. By integrating communication, education, and engagement into the Program's core research activities over the next decade, USGCRP and its member agencies will serve as an unprecedentedly important gateway to credible and authoritative global change scientific information. The Program's education efforts will also support the critical goal of developing a home-grown scientific workforce capable of bridging the physical, chemical, biological, and social sciences, and coordinating that integrated knowledge-base with the engineering skills that are needed to respond to global change challenges and cultivate future research advances.

This Strategic Plan acknowledges several looming challenges in global change research. Among them, the Nation is at risk of experiencing observational gaps that would affect the ability to monitor and understand natural and human-induced variability, due to developmental and launch delays of replacements for aging systems (e.g., Earth Observing System satellites). Also, to achieve the new heights of multimodal integration recommended in this Plan, scientists and engineers will have to overcome the technical challenges of integrating observing and data systems focused on the physical environment with the range of social and ecological observations collected by other means.

Finally, this Plan recognizes that global change is an international concern. Across the Nation and around the world, people are increasingly becoming aware of the need to mitigate effectively the impacts of global change and adapt to those changes that cannot be prevented. The global nature of today's economy—and the speed with which challenges faced in one part of the world can affect others—reinforce the need for a global response based upon the best available science. Social, economic, and political upheaval can result from such manifestations of global change as decreased availability of water, food, and other critical resources that can sweep across regional and national boundaries. Understanding global change and the options for minimizing and managing its risks is important for U.S. national security and for maintaining regional and global stability.

A worldwide issue such as global change also requires international research cooperation. Observations across the globe are crucial to develop the long-term data sets needed to leverage and build upon U.S. investments. Networks of satellite, ocean, atmosphere, and land-based observations are essential to producing the data necessary to test models and advance research that can ultimately protect livelihoods and the environment.

To summarize, looking forward, the USGCRP will work to integrate the physical, chemical, biological, and social sciences; interact with decision makers about research results relevant to their needs; advance communication and interdisciplinary education in global change research; and make effective use of assessment results to inform future research activities. Broadening Federal participation in the Program is also needed, as current agency participants may lack the direct links to and experience with stakeholder communities that are key to developing viable adaptation and mitigation options. The implementation strategy section of the Strategic Plan outlines a path forward to address these and other challenging aspects of the new strategic goals and objectives.

Taken together, the Program envisioned through this Strategic Plan will coordinate the work of Federal agencies more productively than ever, ensuring a more effective global change research effort for the benefit of the Nation.

Box 1. USGCRP Strategic Goals and Objectives

Goal 1. Advance Science: Advance scientific knowledge of the integrated natural and human components of the Earth system.

- *Objective 1.1. Earth System Understanding:* Advance fundamental understanding of the physical, chemical, biological, and human components of the Earth system, and the interactions among them, to improve knowledge of the causes and consequences of global change.

- *Objective 1.2. Science for Adaptation and Mitigation:* Advance understanding of the vulnerability and resilience of integrated human-natural systems and enhance the usability of scientific knowledge in supporting responses to global change.

- *Objective 1.3. Integrated Observations:* Advance capabilities to observe the physical, chemical, biological, and human components of the Earth system over multiple space and time scales to gain fundamental scientific understanding and monitor important variations and trends.

- *Objective 1.4. Integrated Modeling:* Improve and develop advanced models that integrate across the physical, chemical, biological, and human components of the Earth system, including the feedbacks among them, to represent more comprehensively and predict more realistically global change processes.

- *Objective 1.5. Information Management and Sharing:* Advance the capability to collect, store, access, visualize, and share data and information about the integrated Earth system, the vulnerabilities of integrated human-natural systems to global change, and the responses to these vulnerabilities.

Goal 2. Inform Decisions: Provide the scientific basis to inform and enable timely decisions on adaptation and mitigation.

- *Objective 2.1. Inform Adaptation Decisions:* Improve the deployment and accessibility of science to inform adaptation decisions.

- *Objective 2.2. Inform Mitigation Decisions:* Improve the deployment and accessibility of science to inform decisions on mitigation and the mitigation-adaptation interface.

- *Objective 2.3. Enhance Global Change Information:* Develop the tools and scientific basis to enable an integrated system of global change information, informed by sustained, relevant, and timely data to support decision making.

Goal 3. Conduct Sustained Assessments: Build sustained assessment capacity that improves the Nation's ability to understand, anticipate, and respond to global change impacts and vulnerabilities.

- *Objective 3.1. Scientific Integration:* Integrate emerging scientific understanding of the integrated Earth system into assessments and identify critical gaps and limitations in scientific understanding.

- *Objective 3.2. Ongoing Capacity:* Strengthen and evolve ongoing capacity to conduct assessments with accessible, transparent, and consistent processes and broad participation of stakeholders across regions and sectors.

- *Objective 3.3. Inform Responses:* Inform responses to global change with accurate, authoritative, and timely information that is accessible to multiple audiences in multiple formats.

- *Objective 3.4. Evaluate Progress:* Ensure ongoing evaluation of assessment processes and products, and incorporate the findings into an adaptive response for systemic improvement.

Goal 4. Communicate and Educate: Advance communications and education to broaden public understanding of global change and develop the scientific workforce of the future.

- *Objective 4.1. Strengthen Communication and Education Research:* Strengthen the effectiveness of global change communication and education research to enhance practices.

- *Objective 4.2. Reach Diverse Audiences:* Enhance existing and employ emerging tools and resources to inform and educate effectively, providing for information flow in multiple directions.

- *Objective 4.3. Increase Engagement:* Establish effective and sustained engagement to enable a responsive and wholly integrated Program.

- *Objective 4.4. Cultivate Scientific Workforce:* Cultivate a capable, diverse scientific workforce that is knowledgeable about global change.

I. Introduction

The United States Global Change Research Program (USGCRP) advances the collective efforts of 13 U.S. Government agencies that collaboratively help the Nation better understand global change and its impacts.

The rate of global change today—including increased human-induced emissions of heat-trapping gases, disruptions of natural ecological and geochemical cycles, changing patterns of land use and associated changes in climate, oceans, and the distribution of species over the planet—far exceeds anything observed and documented in human history. Decision makers across the Nation and around the world are asking scientists for clear and reliable information on how these changes will affect individuals, communities, and economies, and how best to respond to those likely impacts. While global change poses a number of serious challenges, a failure to anticipate and manage those challenges can only amplify the threat to prosperity and security in the United States and around the world. By contrast, the development and implementation of effective responses can not only prevent some of the worst potential impacts of global change but also create new opportunities for economic growth and societal well-being.

Making the best decisions with regard to global change will depend on a well-grounded understanding of the Earth system and the changes taking place within it. The Earth system includes the complex and interrelated physical, chemical, biological, and human interactions across the land, ocean, and atmosphere. For example, a deeper understanding of the El Niño Southern Oscillation (**Box 13**), growing seasons (**Box 28**), and long-term climate variations can provide valuable information to farmers who need to adjust crop management as planting seasons, growing zones, and pest and weed ranges change. The defense and intelligence communities need to assess the implications of long-term climate change on national security, including, for example, the threats that natural hazards may pose to military bases (**Box 7**). Healthcare providers must prepare for more severe heat waves and outbreaks of diseases previously uncommon in their regions (**Box 12**). Private-sector insurers and the construction industry must account for shifting weather extremes as they assess future financial risks and appropriate building techniques (**Box 27**). Municipal governments and inhabitants of coastal cities need to understand the implications of, and prepare for, sea-level rise (**Box 26**). Additionally, many regions of the country need information about changing freshwater availability, ways to meet energy demands, and the potential for more frequent extreme events including heat waves, storms, floods, droughts, and fires.

These growing needs exist in the context of increasing demand for Earth's resources, including food, fiber, energy, and water—needs that are putting new pressure on the critical services that natural systems provide, such as freshwater supply, natural waste recycling, water purification, pollination, flood

> ### Box 2. Global Change Meaning
>
> Global change means changes in the global environment (including alterations in climate, land productivity, oceans or other water resources, atmospheric chemistry, and ecological systems) that may alter the capacity of the Earth to sustain life. 'Global change research' means study, monitoring, assessment, prediction, and information management activities to describe and understand: A. the interactive physical, chemical, and biological processes that regulate the total Earth system; B. the unique environment that the Earth provides for life; C. changes that are occurring in the Earth system; and D. the manner in which such system, environment, and changes are influenced by human actions.
>
> - The Global Change Research Act of 1990

control, and recreation. Leaders and decision makers across the Nation need and appropriately expect trustworthy scientific information that can point to environmentally sustainable solutions to these synergistic pressures while promoting economic growth.

USGCRP (**Box 3**)—which began as a Presidential Initiative in 1989, was codified in law by Congress in 1990, and has been sustained through each successive administration—was created expressly to address these kinds of challenges. During it's more than two decades of existence it has coordinated Federal investments in global change science to maximize efficiencies and ensure the continuity of a comprehensive research portfolio. Throughout this time period, USGCRP and its member agencies —in collaboration with partners in industry, academia, and state, tribal, local, and foreign governments—has: (1) created and maintained a mix of atmospheric, oceanic, land, and space-based observing systems; (2) gained new theoretical knowledge of Earth system processes; (3) advanced understanding of the complexity of the Earth system through predictive modeling; (4) promoted advances in computational capabilities, data management, and information sharing; and (5) developed and harnessed an expert scientific workforce. These activities have proven critical to improving our scientific understanding of the rich interconnections and feedbacks within the Earth system; the significant role of human activities in climate change; and the current and potential future rates, magnitudes, and impacts of this change. Federal research coordinated through USGCRP stands today as the foundation of the Nation's current understanding of these issues.[2]

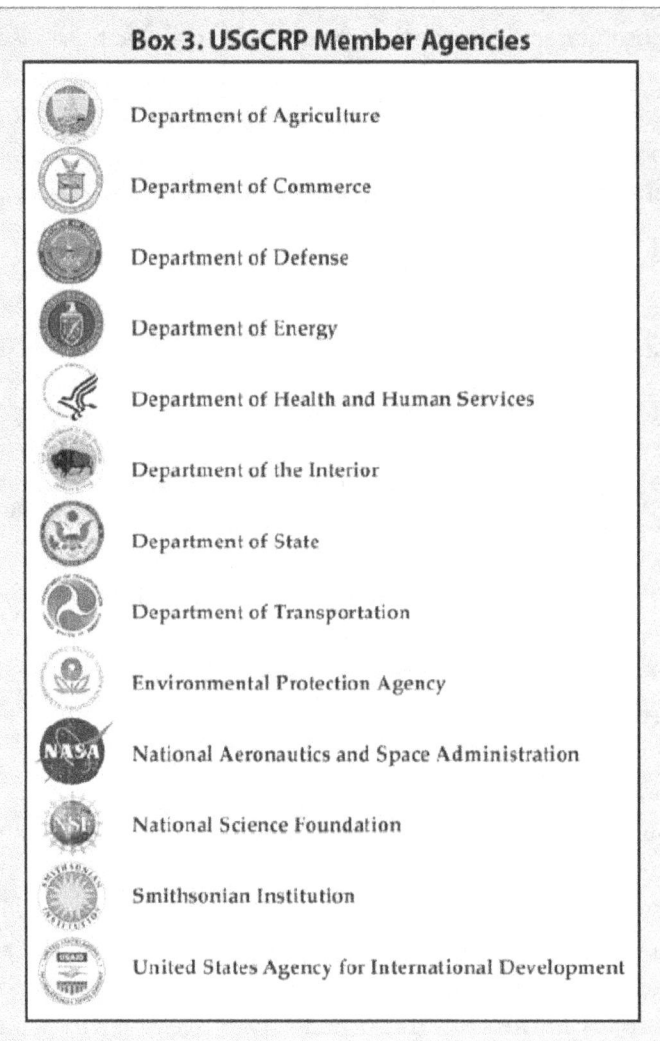

Box 3. USGCRP Member Agencies

Department of Agriculture

Department of Commerce

Department of Defense

Department of Energy

Department of Health and Human Services

Department of the Interior

Department of State

Department of Transportation

Environmental Protection Agency

National Aeronautics and Space Administration

National Science Foundation

Smithsonian Institution

United States Agency for International Development

The 2012–2021 Strategic Plan describes a Program that builds upon core USGCRP science capabilities to strengthen and expand the fundamental understanding of climate change and its interactions with other critical drivers of global change, such as land-use change, the alteration of key carbon, water, and nitrogen cycles, and biodiversity loss. Society is placing increasing demands on the scientific community for timely information about global change that can be applied directly to planning, management,

2. National Research Council. Earth Science and Applications from Space: National Imperatives for the Next Decade and Beyond. Washington, D.C.: National Academies Press, 2007.

and policymaking. Drawing on fundamental knowledge built over the last 20 years, USGCRP is in an unparalleled position to effectively and authoritatively deliver new information about the changing Earth system that decision makers across the Nation will need for the future.

This Strategic Plan describes a Program that creates new scientific knowledge and makes this knowledge more readily available and usable in decision making. The Program will build on member agencies' strengths in scientific measurement and modeling; incorporate new knowledge about decision making under conditions of uncertainty; and apply improved methods for iterative, risk-based planning. The Strategic Plan emphasizes greater coordination across the breadth of USGCRP activities, including more effective collaboration among researchers in the natural and social sciences, increased interagency cooperation to sustain ongoing assessments of global change impacts, and robust dialogues with diverse audiences to enhance communication of scientific knowledge.

The Federal government has an important role with regard to global change—not just as a supporter of scientific research but also as an entity uniquely capable of providing researchers and decision makers with the best scientific information to manage global change risks. This Strategic Plan embraces historically successful USGCRP activities and proposes new strategies to meet the needs of decision makers over the next decade. Successful implementation of this Plan will require that USGCRP leverage the full and varied capabilities and missions of its Federal member agencies, as well as build new partnerships with agencies that have not been directly involved with USGCRP in the past.

The speed with which challenges faced in one part of the world can affect other parts in today's global economy reinforces the need for a timely and coordinated international response to global change. At the same time, not all countries, communities, and institutions will be equally affected, or equally ready or able to adapt. Nor will every consequence of global change be detrimental to everyone. To support the many types of responses to global change needed locally, regionally, nationally, and internationally, decision makers will need more detailed information about global change, improved assessments of the risks and the opportunities posed by that change, and a more fine-grained breakdown of the differences in vulnerability among people and places. This Strategic Plan offers a roadmap to meeting these needs.

Chapter II of this Plan provides an overview of the new vision and mission for the Program to meet future challenges. Chapter III discusses in detail the goals and objectives relating to scientific activities, decision support, assessments, and expanding educational and communication efforts over the next decade. Chapter IV discusses coordination with other nations and international organizations. Finally, Chapter V outlines a strategy for implementing the Strategic Plan.

Box 4. Twenty Years of Progress in Advancing Scientific Knowledge of Global Change

The USGCRP delivers a variety of publications that highlight scientific advances pertaining to global change. In addition to detailing scientific progress, USGCRP products illustrate the impacts of global change and highlight the Nation's response to these changes. As mandated by Congress, the USGCRP produces regular assessments of global change and annual reports showcasing the Program's progress in achieving its annual goals. Below are some descriptions of recent USGCRP publications.

A 2009 USGCRP publication, *Global Climate Change Impacts in the U.S.*, summarizes the science and impacts of climate change in the U.S. This report provides easily digestible key messages and scientific findings to better inform public and private decision making at all levels. The report focuses on the impacts of global change on human health, climate variability, and water resources, among other areas. It shows the effects of global change on different regions of the U.S. and on various aspects of society and the economy, such as energy, water, agriculture, and health. This publication fulfills a statutory mandate to assess the scientific knowledge of the impacts, risks and vulnerabilities associated with a changing global climate, in support of decision making across the United States.[3]

Figure: Cover of "Global Climate Change Impacts in the United States"

Figure: Selected covers from Synthesis and Assessment Products

---

3. Also available interactively at http://www.globalchange.gov/what-we-do/assessments/previous-assessments/global-climate-change-impacts-in-the-us-2009.

4. For more information, visit http://library.globalchange.gov

USGCRP agencies also led the production of 21 Synthesis and Assessment Products (SAPs). These reports provide research results that focus on relevant science topics and aim to inform discussions and decision making regarding climate variability and change. The reports target stakeholders including policy makers, resource managers, the media, and the general public.

Since 1989, USGCRP has produced an annual report that summarizes recent programmatic achievements, near-term plans, and progress in implementing long-term goals. *Our Changing Planet* compiles recent research of USGCRP agencies on global change for the Congress, responding to the requirements of the U.S. Global Change Research Act of 1990 for an annual report on "Federal global change research priorities, policies, and programs."The annual report also provides an overview of recent and near-term expenditures and of requested funding.

Figure: Cover Pages of Recent Our Changing Planet Reports

USGCRP products are available and free to the public through the USGCRP Resource Library (previously known as the Global Change Research Information Office, GCRIO). The Resource Library provides access to data and information on climate change research, adaptation and mitigation strategies and technologies, and global change-related educational resources on behalf of the USGCRP.[4]

Illustrative Examples of Program Accomplishments and Future Directions

The Strategic Plan illustrates selected past accomplishments from, and future directions for, USGCRP research. For example, the Program calls for periodic assessments of climate and global change, annual reports on the Program's accomplishments, and reports on topics ranging from climate literacy to a synthesis and assessment of abrupt climate change (**Box 4**). Topical boxes placed throughout the document demonstrate diverse and distinct USGCRP outcomes and activities:

- (Box 7) USGCRP research used in the 2010 Quadrennial Defense Review, a primary source of information on how expected climate change will affect the Department of Defense

- (Box 10) Carbon dioxide emissions changing the chemistry of seawater, resulting in ocean acidification, an effect that may result in damage to sea creatures and the ocean food web

- (Box 11) Plant and animal species habitats shift, often poleward and upward in elevation, in response to recent climate change affecting entire ecosystems

- (Boxes 13 and 22) Natural oscillations resulting in year-to-year and decade-to-decade variations in regional climate worldwide, and research on alterations in natural variability as a result of climate change

- (Box 14) Research on integrated observational systems, with models from economists, other social scientists, and natural scientists, to help decision makers track the effects of climate change on food, energy, and water production

- (Box 15) A decades-long trend in higher sea levels revealed by observations, and research to advance the models scientists and planners use to project future sea-level rise to document long-term variability

- (Box 16) Research to allow water resource decision makers to better understand the interactions between changes in climate and changing patterns in regional precipitation, runoff, and drought

- (Box 17) Best practices for building community and ecosystem resilience to the impacts of declining sea ice

- (Box 20) Long-term observations, which are crucial to understanding of global changes and their effects, including data on increasing forest fires and drought

- (Box 21) Research using Integrated Assessment Models, which include coupled natural components and human-related components

- (Box 23) An interagency initiative to build a new Global Change Information System, providing timely and relevant data and information to stakeholders and the public

- (Box 25) Urban adaptation informed by science that helped Chicago develop a response to projected higher temperatures, potential flooding, and steps for energy management

- (Box 26) A tool for communities to plan for sea-level rise and coastal flooding

- (Box 27) Information for the construction industry that allows accounting for climate change

- (Box 28) Coordinated efforts that, through observations, crop- and forest-growth models, and regional climate models, provide authoritative information to officials and tools for use by farmers and landowners

- (Box 31) Data and information to assist New York City with city planning in the face of projected sea-level rise

- (Box 32) Identification of opportunities for conservation and restoration to assist state, Federal, tribal, and nongovernmental organizations in responding to USGCRP research outcomes

- (Box 33) Scientific participation in international assessments, where U S. scientists play an important role in analyzing the current state of science and adaptation efforts worldwide

- (Box 35) Development of *Climate Literacy: The Essential Principles of Climate Science (2009)*, a resource for teachers, students, and community leaders to use as a topic for discussion within local communities, and as a guide for developing informal learning resources and science curriculum standards

- (Box 36) Use of informal environments for science learning, such as community-educator partnerships and direct engagements with diverse audiences

- (Box 37) Public engagement in research observations through the USA National Phenology Network, which monitors plants, animals, and landscapes and provides key data to uncover trends and changes on a national scale

- (Box 38) Research to advance understanding of the many interacting elements of the carbon cycle, which is critical to decision making regarding, for example, emissions from cars and power plants, reversing deforestation, and capturing and storing carbon

- (Box 39) International cooperation and how environmental change at global and regional scales requires greater scientific expertise, technological capabilities, and resources than any one country can provide

Box 5. Where Have All the Songbirds Gone?

Thirty years ago, that question sparked a long-term research study on migratory birds that has created deeper understanding of the impact of global change on biodiversity. The work sparked new modeling capabilities, adaptation planning, reforestation efforts, and new technologies to track and monitor even very small animals.

Global change is affecting fundamental aspects of the biology of many species including their migratory behavior, breeding distributions, and even evolutionary processes. The use of increasingly sophisticated mapping, tracking, and molecular techniques is vital to providing key scientific knowledge for conservation, sustainable use, and effective management. International research and conservation cooperation is necessary to understand and mitigate the effects of global change on migratory species.

Migratory species range from butterflies to antelope to whales to birds, and vary widely in physical characteristics, habitat, and threats to their existence. Migratory animals are important for many reasons—as food, as pollinators, for intrinsic enjoyment—but they also can carry infectious diseases and agricultural pests. The geographic link between individuals and populations throughout a complete annual cycle—known as migratory connectivity—is key to understanding them in all their guises. Fundamental to emerging understanding is the knowledge of the breeding, migration, and winter stages of species, and developing an understanding of events in one period (e.g., winter, year 1) that may influence events in subsequent periods (summer, year 2).

The study of migratory connectivity enables the understanding of species vulnerability to climate change throughout the annual cycle and geographic range of a migratory species. Understanding migratory connectivity is also essential for minimizing the impacts of human activities, such as the siting of energy projects (wind turbines, pipelines, and dams). For most species, the degree of migratory connectivity remains unknown.

Connectivity research has discovered that many species of migratory birds overwinter in habitats that are being degraded and this has important consequences for their health and fitness. For example, it was found that migrants wintering on coffee farms with shade trees fared better than those wintering on farms without shade trees. This research led to the development of the mitigation assistance technique known as shade grown coffee and the Bird Friendly® coffee program, an effort to provide forested sanctuaries for migratory birds while providing agricultural opportunities to local citizens. Shade grown cacao, rice farming, and semi-forested cattle pastures are other tropical agroforestry projects that are Bird Friendly® and demonstrate the expanding impact of this research.

Another study on the American Redstart examined how events on the bird's tropical wintering grounds influence events thousands of miles to the north. The study, which was conducted at the Font Hill Nature Reserve in Jamaica, used stable carbon isotopes in red-blood cells to connect events throughout the annual cycle and confirmed that conditions of the wintering habitat interacted with climate extremes affecting the probability of survival during migration and the reproductive success of birds.

Improving technology allows a new approach to measuring migratory connectivity using transmitters on individuals throughout their annual cycle. This allows investigators to place animal movements in larger contexts. Bringing data on the movements of individual organisms into concert with satellite-derived variables of climate, vegetation, and land cover, opens new doors. It improves understanding of the interactions between global change and health of migratory species. USGCRP agencies, such as National Aeronautics and Space Administration (NASA), National Oceanic and Atmospheric Administration (NOAA), and U.S. Geological Survey (USGS), maintain databases of satellite products as well as georeferenced and time-stamped species inventories (Smithsonian, USFWS, NOAA, and USGS). Efforts to bring these types of information together, along with models that link environmental patterns to species, are underway. An International Cooperation for Animal Research Using Space (ICARUS) initiative is being developed. Also promising is the development of Internet-based tools such as Movebank, a repository for international organismal movement data across space and time. These efforts are being championed by an important new effort called The Migratory Connectivity Project.[5]

Migratory species also may carry diseases that animals pass to humans, including West Nile virus and avian flu. Climate change in turn changes the range of host organisms. Public health efforts also must change to reflect the new realities of an increased probability of introduced zoonotic pathogens. The problem is challenging because it requires an integrated understanding from diverse fields from immunology to ornithology, and also because no single agency or group is currently equipped to cope with these challenges.

---

5. For more information on the Migratory Connectivity Project, visit http://www.migratoryconnectivityproject.org/.

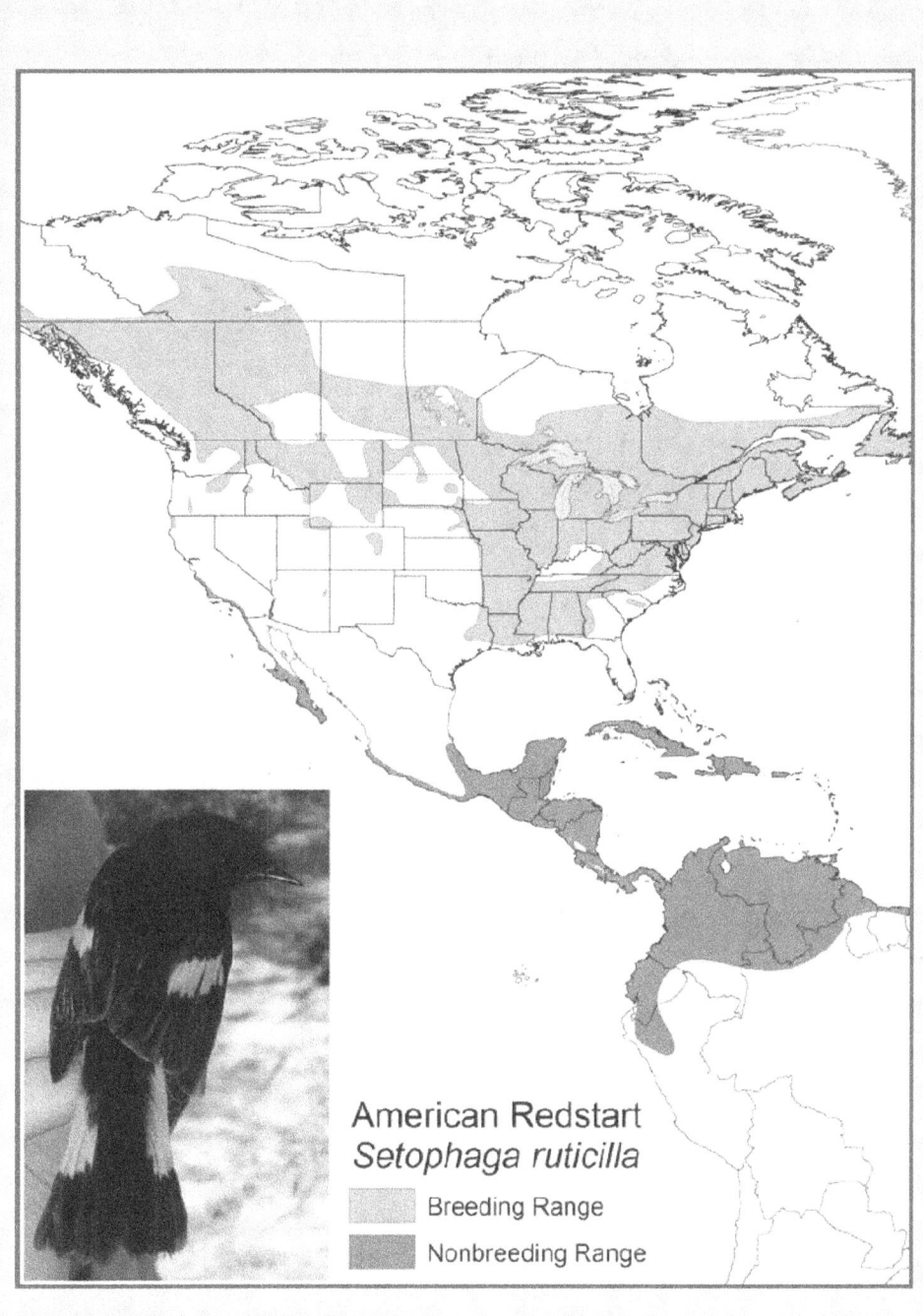

American Redstart
Setophaga ruticilla

Breeding Range
Nonbreeding Range

Figure: The American redstart (Setophaga ruticilla) is a long distance Neotropical-Nearctic migratory bird. It breeds in the United States and Canada (Yellow) between the months of May and early August and spends the majority of its annual cycle on the non-breeding grounds in Middle America, the Caribbean and northern South America (green). Image courtesy of Peter P. Marra.

II. Framework for USGCRP

USGCRP Vision and Mission

> **Vision:** *A Nation, globally engaged and guided by science, meeting the challenges of climate and global change.*
>
> **Mission:** *To build a knowledge base that informs human responses to climate and global change through coordinated and integrated Federal programs of research, education, communication, and decision support.*

The Program's vision reflects the urgent challenges discussed in the Introduction, and the central role of U.S. science in addressing those challenges. The mission statement articulates the Program's role in addressing the mandated scope of the Global Change Research Act over the next decade. Together they form a foundation for this Strategic Plan, which emphasizes better integration of social, ecological, and physical sciences to understand changing conditions, increased utilization of scientific information and knowledge, and better communication and education. This more integrated approach requires enhanced coordination among the member agencies and will build on the strong partnerships already in place. It also requires the Program to expand relationships beyond its current membership, to better understand and respond to the science needs of the agencies and their stakeholders, and to increase the use of USGCRP science in the Nation's response to global change.

The Strategic Plan is based on the Program's previous accomplishments in monitoring and understanding global change, the likely future impacts of global change, and their relevance to society's needs. Over the next decade, USGCRP will maintain these strengths and build on the Program's initial efforts in decision support to increase the impact of USGCRP science. The Program will enhance its current capabilities to better assess, understand, and integrate stakeholder science needs into its planning, and to provide global change assessments and information in ways that are more useful for decision making. These directions reflect the Program's emphasis on developing and sharing information that is useable and useful. Throughout the Strategic Plan, the Program focuses on the interaction between climate change and other aspects of global change, such as land-use change, loss of biodiversity, changing hydrological conditions, and alteration of key biogeochemical cycles.

This Strategic Plan is meant to guide USGCRP strategic directions for the next 10 years. It is not a detailed plan for programmatic activities, which will evolve considerably over the decade. Rather, it provides guiding principles and mechanisms for implementing and linking the Strategic Plan to intermediate and near-term priorities and activities. In implementing the Strategic Plan, USGCRP will continue to uphold principles of intellectual rigor, transparency, accessibility, and traceability. In addressing major scientific challenges, the Program will mobilize the best scientific skills at home and abroad, use merit review processes to develop priorities, and use peer review to ensure the quality and accuracy of products.

This chapter provides a brief overview of the USGCRP and key elements that frame the goals and objectives of the Strategic Plan. See Chapter V for more detailed material on Program structure, governance, and implementation.

Overview

The USGCRP is a confederation of the research components of 13 Federal departments and agencies. These 13 departments and agencies carry out research and maintain and develop capabilities that support the Nation's response to global change, in coordination with the Subcommittee on Global Change Research (SGCR). The SGCR reports to the Committee on Environment, Natural Resources, and Sustainability (CENRS), which is part of the National Science and Technology Council (NSTC) (**Box 6**), and provides coordination with other parts of that structure, including other CENRS subcommittees with mandates that relate to global change.

The SGCR coordinates interagency activities through the USGCRP National Coordination Office (NCO) and interagency working groups (IWGs). Generally, the IWGs correspond to program functions and are designed to bring agencies together to plan and develop coordinated activities, implement joint activities, and identify and fill gaps in the Program's plans. They allow public officials to communicate with each other on emerging directions within their agencies, on their stakeholder needs, and on best practices learned from agency activities. Together, these functions allow the agencies to work in a more coordinated and effective manner. The Program will continue to draw from and leverage agency strengths in achieving the collective USGCRP Strategic Plan goals and objectives.

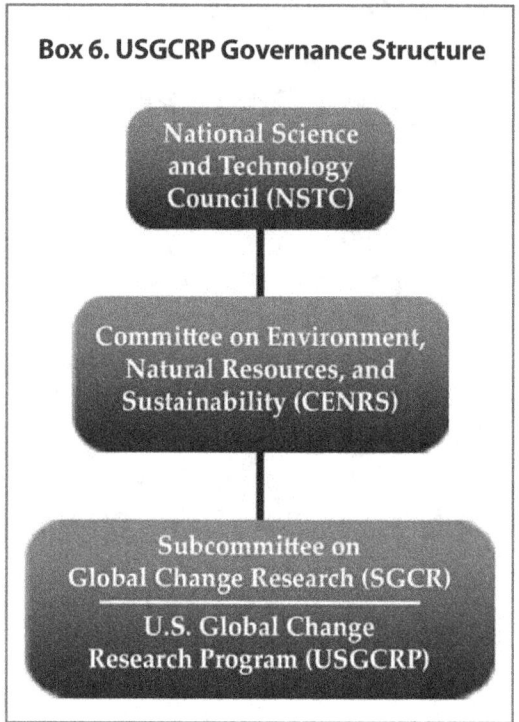

Box 6. USGCRP Governance Structure

National Science and Technology Council (NSTC)

Committee on Environment, Natural Resources, and Sustainability (CENRS)

Subcommittee on Global Change Research (SGCR)

U.S. Global Change Research Program (USGCRP)

In this document, the phrase "USGCRP agencies" is used when referring to research and operations carried out by the 13 member agencies to implement priorities linked to USGCRP. "USGCRP" and "the Program" are used interchangeably when referring to activities that require coordinated planning for agency implementation, as well as the planning, coordination or integration functions themselves carried out by the SGCR, the IWGs, and the NCO. When referring to coordination activities carried out by only one part of the Program, such as the NCO, that entity is identified by name.

The Program's mission will be implemented by USGCRP agencies, scientific staff in agency and contractor laboratories, and agency grant recipients. The USGCRP investments in activities such as observations and monitoring, information services, research and modeling, assessment, communications, and outreach totaled about $2 billion in Fiscal Year (FY) 2010. The USGCRP also builds on investments made by the agencies that are not included in this total. Results from prior USGCRP programs and activities are highlighted in the Introduction and in boxes throughout this Strategic Plan. Outcomes from these activities, along with the investments made by USGCRP agencies, are summarized on a regular basis in the Program's annual report to Congress, *Our Changing Planet*. USGCRP priorities also have the potential to encourage and inspire cooperative efforts by state and local governments, the academic community, and industry, as well as Federal entities not included formally in the USGCRP.

The Program's stakeholders are critical to success. USGCRP agencies interact with a wide variety of groups around the world including international, national, state, tribal, and local governments, businesses, professional and other nonprofit organizations, the scientific community, and the public. Each contributes to USGCRP's ability to carry out its mission. Through dialogue with the agencies, stakeholders communicate their information needs to the Program, helping to shape Program directions and priorities and collectively advance the understanding of global change. In turn, USGCRP strengthens its ability to better communicate global change information to stakeholders to advance their ability to make informed decisions about the changes and challenges they face.

Framework for the New USGCRP

Interlinking goals, unifying themes, and activities that allow simultaneous progress on multiple goals provide the framework for an integrated USGCRP. This framework emphasizes the interdisciplinary approach that is needed for future success and provides direction for expanded areas of the Program.

A detailed discussion of USGCRP objectives and activities linked to the four goals below follows in Chapter III. The goals are designed to build from and support each other in achieving an integrated program.

Goal 1. Advance Science: Advance scientific knowledge of the integrated natural and human components of the Earth system. This goal encompasses the research, including integrated observations and modeling, that is necessary to better understand the behavior and interactions of different aspects of the Earth system (including the human component) and their response to global change. This goal builds on USGCRP's strong research tradition and provides the foundation for the other three goals, which in turn will help shape future research priorities.

Goal 2. Inform Decisions: Provide the scientific basis to inform and enable timely decisions on adaptation and mitigation. USGCRP and member agencies will emphasize translating research (from Goal 1 and other sources) into formats and results that are policy relevant, useable, and accessible to decision makers. The Program also is expanding the ability to provide global change information and tools that the public and private sectors need to make decisions**.**

Goal 3. Conduct Sustained Assessments: Build sustained assessment capacity that improves the Nation's ability to understand, anticipate, and respond to global change impacts and vulnerabilities. USGCRP will conduct and participate in national and international assessments to evaluate the current state of the science and likely future scenarios of global change and their impacts, and evaluate how effectively science is being used to support the Nation's response to change. It will also build a standing capacity to conduct national assessments and support those at regional levels. Together, Goals 2 and 3 will evaluate progress in responding to change and identify science and stakeholder needs for further progress. The Program will use this regular assessment to inform its priorities.

Goal 4. Communicate and Educate: **Advance communications and education to broaden public understanding of global change and develop the scientific workforce of the future**. USGCRP will make its research results available to stakeholders and provide information to citizens in ways that are relevant to their lives and needs. The Program and USGCRP agencies will adopt, develop, and share best practices in communication that enhance stakeholder engagement. Educational efforts will support development of a scientific workforce able to use global change knowledge in their careers to support the Nation's response to global change.

Unifying Themes

There are a number of ideas that track across multiple goals of the Strategic Plan, and provide unifying themes and focus for the Program:

Providing Knowledge on Scales Appropriate for Decision Making. A key unifying idea of this Strategic Plan is to acquire and use scientific knowledge about global change at the spatial and temporal scales on which planning, management, and policy decisions are made. Improvements in global and regional scale models are necessary to meet this need. The Program will develop additional capacity for modeling Earth's climate system on seasonal, annual, and decadal scales, in a context that includes both natural and human systems needed for decision making. Models will address gradual changes in means, as well as potentially larger variations in the resulting distribution of extreme events, and even greater changes associated with thresholds and tipping points. The Program will coordinate research on regions where the effects of global change will be most acutely felt or where feedback effects are most significant.

Incorporating Social and Biological Sciences. This Strategic Plan highlights the importance of increased integration of the physical, social, and biological sciences to better understand the impact of global change on ecosystems and the services they provide, as well as how humans drive and respond to global change. Integrated biological research at the population, species, community and ecosystem levels is critical to understanding, for example, the impacts of global change on ecosystem services and biodiversity. Contributions from social and behavioral sciences are essential to identifying the spatial distribution of people and global change issues, understanding decisions, managing risks, and formulating policy options in the face of incomplete information. This new knowledge must go beyond the direct application, such as understanding decisions, to the broader scientific knowledge that relates the cognition and behavior of individuals, families, and businesses to their environmental setting. Harnessing the benefit of such integration will require attention to the observational and information management needs in the biological and social sciences as they tie to global change. This Strategic Plan also notes the workforce challenges and opportunities for better incorporation of social scientists into the Program.

Enabling Responses to Global Change via Iterative Risk Management. USGCRP has an important role to play in providing information useful for iterative risk management. Iterative risk management is an adaptive process of identifying risks and response options, advancing a portfolio of actions that emphasize risk reduction across a range of likely future conditions, and revising responses to reflect new knowledge. In particular, USGCRP's role will be to support research and development that provides the knowledge needed to improve response options to global change. As options are selected and implemented, the Program will monitor and assess progress being made through the Nation's response efforts and the science needed to support further progress. The scientific expertise mobilized by USGCRP will develop the knowledge necessary to prepare and evaluate responses to change, and to evaluate consequences, both intended and unintended.

Cross-Linking Activities

In addition to themes that link the goals and objectives of this Strategic Plan, there are activities that simultaneously benefit multiple goals. The topics listed are discussed under specific objectives in Chapter III, but connectivity across the goals is briefly highlighted here.

Enhance Information Management and Sharing. Creating and sharing knowledge, data, and projections of likely future conditions is essential to researchers, resource managers, decision makers, educators, and the public. The Program will leverage information tools, services, and portals from the USGCRP agencies to develop a global change information system, a "one-stop shop" for accessing global change data and information (**Box 23**). Through its members, the Program will also develop a virtual environment for collaboration among researchers and educators, providing enhanced capabilities in areas such as data assimilation, community models, and visualization.

Enable a High Capability for Integrated Observations and Modeling. Integrated modeling and observations are essential approaches for USGCRP. Together, they provide the scaffolding needed to develop scenarios of likely future conditions, characterize their uncertainties, understand changes over time, and investigate the likely consequences of action (and inaction) in response to global change. The USGCRP strategy for sustaining key observational capability will emphasize continued investment in, and development of, observations in societal benefit areas that are most important for answering critical questions in global change research. These benefit areas are at the intersection of climate change with agriculture, biodiversity, disasters, ecology, energy, human health, oceans, water, and weather. The USGCRP agencies will work with the National Research Council and other CENRS entities such as U.S. Group on Earth Observations (**Box 18**) in developing plans to sustain these essential observations, fill critical observational gaps in key regions and disciplines (including biological and societal), improve data quality where necessary to improve fundamental process understanding and model predictability, and reduce uncertainties.

Box 7. Department of Defense and the Use of Climate Change Science

USGCRP-produced information was cited in the U.S. Department of Defense's (DoD) 2010 Quadrennial Defense Review as a primary source of information on expected climate change that would affect the DoD by shaping its future operating environment, roles, and missions. In addition, assessments conducted by the intelligence community indicate that climate change could have significant geopolitical impacts around the world by contributing to poverty, environmental degradation, and the further weakening of fragile governments. Although climate change alone does not cause conflict, it may act as an accelerant of instability or conflict and may place a burden to respond on civilian institutions and militaries around the world. The intelligence community also judged that more than 30 U.S. military installations faced increased risk from rising sea levels. Finally, extreme weather events may lead to increased demands for defense support to civil authorities for humanitarian assistance or disaster response both within the United States and overseas.

The U.S. Navy and Coast Guard are actively cooperating on Arctic issues. The U.S. Coast Guard participates in Arctic Domain Awareness flights that take place every two weeks from mid-spring to mid-fall. The flights collect scientific information on carbon dioxide and methane in the atmosphere, as well as monitor maritime traffic in the U.S. Arctic maritime environment.

Figure: Photo taken September 23, 2010, from loading ramp of a U.S. Coast Guard C-130 over the Beaufort Sea. Image courtesy of CDR B. McBride.

Increase Proactive Engagement and Partnerships. To maximize the benefit of USGCRP, the Program will strengthen its partnerships across multiple levels of government, including engaging a broader cross section within USGCRP agencies and with agencies currently outside of USGCRP, where department and agency missions directly relate to Program activities. USGCRP also will build appropriate relationships with private foundations, nongovernmental organizations, and business sectors to inform USGCRP planning, and extend the reach and utility of its research and capabilities. The Program will establish a framework that engenders effective dialogue with policy and decision makers in both public and private sectors.

Leverage International Leadership. In the Global Change Research Act, Congress recognized the importance of international cooperation to global change research and mandated a role for USGCRP in the international community. The Program engages in international cooperation because it enhances and complements the strengths, interests, and needs of USGCRP and its partner agencies. The challenges and opportunities that USGCRP faces are global in scope and are larger than what the United States can achieve on its own. International engagement is important in all fields of science, but it is indispensable for the science of USGCRP. Global observing systems are essential to global change research and require international partnerships. Field-based campaigns often require international partnership. USGCRP works with sister interagency entities such as the U.S. Group on Earth Observations (USGEO) and the Interagency Working Group on Digital Data which help set the standards and coordination of Earth observation data in a long-term, durable, and usable fashion. U.S. and international efforts together provide the information and capabilities needed by scientists and institutions in developing countries as they respond to global change. More detailed information about coordinating USGCRP global change research activities with other nations and international organizations is provided in Chapter IV.

Develop the Scientific Workforce for the Future. Research to support adaptation and mitigation strategies, its translation for decision makers, and assessment of its effectiveness are all areas requiring specialized skills and a trained workforce. USGCRP agencies will use their relationships with academia to promote the interdisciplinary education at undergraduate and graduate levels needed for a professional and technical workforce in areas directly related to global change.

The next chapter provides a detailed look at the four goals and their objectives. It outlines key areas of research and new capabilities for the next decade to support the country's response to global change. Chapter IV discusses USGCRP coordination with other nations and international organizations. Chapter V outlines guidelines the Program will use in implementing these priorities over the next ten years.

III. Goals and Objectives

This chapter develops the scientific framework for the goals and objectives of the Strategic Plan. It emphasizes "fundamental, use-inspired research" and the development of and integration across Program capabilities needed to conduct this research, share results, assess progress, and engage with decision makers and stakeholders. In the next decade, the Program will strive to foster the iterative and collaborative dialogue between science and society needed to develop the scientific foundation for understanding and managing the risks of global change in the areas of greatest societal need.

The goals themselves align with key areas identified in different National Research Council reports rather than with traditional disciplinary science topics. Scientific accomplishments in specific areas and future scientific directions are highlighted in the text and in boxes throughout the Strategic Plan.

The goals and objectives are written as discrete sections, but are intended to operate as a cohesive set. For example, Objectives 1.1 (Earth System Understanding) and 1.2 (Science for Adaptation and Mitigation) put forward the research areas that will provide the outcomes and products necessary to accomplish all the other goals. Similarly, needed advances in integrated observations and integrated modeling, as well as a comprehensive strategy for information management and sharing including the development of a new USGCRP Global Change Information System (**Box 23**), are developed in detail under Goal 1 but thread throughout the subsequent goals. The processes for understanding societal needs for research in the next decade, and the opportunities for enhancing Program capacity in new research areas, are articulated in Goals 2, 3, and 4. While each goal mentions the type of scientific workforce needed for its success, the focused workforce discussion is under Goal 4.

As part of a decadal plan, the goals and objectives are described at a strategic level; approaches to implementation planning needed to realize these strategic goals and objectives are discussed in Chapter V. Finally, while this document draws upon the latest global change research, it is not intended to be a research report. As a result, this document periodically references major synthesis documents such as National Research Council reports, but usually not individual science papers.

Goal 1: Advance Science

Advance scientific knowledge of the integrated natural and human components of the Earth system

Scientific knowledge of the integrated Earth system is the foundation for responding effectively to global change. In the next decade, USGCRP and its member agencies will advance fundamental, use-inspired research (**Box 8**) that contributes to both improved understanding and effective decision making. To serve society in meeting present and future challenges, this research program will be built on two principles. The first is to improve fundamental scientific understanding of the integrated natural and human components of the Earth system. The second principle is to focus on the essential science needs for reducing ecological and societal vulnerability to global change by increasing resilience and helping the Nation manage risk through well-informed responses.

This Strategic Plan defines a research program for USGCRP that acknowledges the complexity of global change as both a scientific and societal challenge. To meet this challenge, the research program embraces multiple forms of integration across the components of the Earth system (including people), across observations and modeling, across space and time, across scientific disciplines, across domestic and international partnerships, and across the capabilities of science and the needs of stakeholders.

The Program will accomplish this first Strategic Plan goal through the pursuit of five objectives:

Objective 1.1 Earth System Understanding:
Advance fundamental understanding of the physical, chemical, biological, and human components of the Earth system, and the interactions among them, to improve knowledge of the causes and consequences of global change.

Objective 1.2 Science for Adaptation and Mitigation:
Advance understanding of the vulnerability and resilience of integrated human-natural systems and enhance the usability of scientific knowledge in supporting responses to global change.

Objective 1.3 Integrated Observations:
Advance capabilities to observe the physical, chemical, biological, and human components of the Earth system over multiple space and time scales to gain fundamental scientific understanding and monitor important variations and trends.

> **Box 8. Fundamental, Use-Inspired Research**
>
> Climate change research should focus on fundamental, use-inspired research. This report recognizes the need for scientific research to improve understanding of climate change and to assist in decision making related to climate change. In categorizing these types of scientific research, we found that terms such as "pure," "basic," "applied," and "curiosity driven" have different definitions across communities. These terms are as likely to cause confusion as to advance consensus, and are of limited value in discussing climate change. More compelling, however, is the categorization offered by Stokes [6], who argues that two questions should be asked of a research topic: Does it contribute to fundamental understanding? Can it be expected to be useful? Research that can answer yes to these questions, or "fundamental, use-inspired research," warrants special priority in the realm of climate change research.
>
> *National Research Council (2010): America's Climate Choices: Advancing the Science of Climate Change*

Objective 1.4 Integrated Modeling:
Improve and develop advanced models that integrate across the physical, chemical, biological, and human components of the Earth system, including the feedbacks among them, to represent more comprehensively and predict more realistically global change processes.

Objective 1.5 Information Management and Sharing:
Advance the capability to collect, store, access, visualize, and share data and information about the integrated Earth system, the vulnerabilities of integrated human-natural systems to global change, and the responses to these vulnerabilities.

Although these five objectives are defined distinctly and discussed separately, they describe one integrated body of knowledge and practice. Objectives 1.1 and 1.2 respectively define the two-fold

---

6. Stokes, D. E. 1997. *Pasteur's quadrant: Basic science and technological innovation.* Washington, D.C.: Brookings Institution Press.

intellectual core of the strategy for advancing USGCRP science in the next decade: seeking answers to fundamental scientific questions about the integrated Earth system and harnessing that improved scientific understanding to support the development of actions in response to global change.

Objective 1.1 describes, very broadly, the research directions for achieving a deeper, more fundamental understanding of the physical, chemical, biological, and human components of the Earth system, and the richness of behaviors that result from their interaction with each other. Key elements include broadening the Program's focus to consider an expanded range of global change dimensions and their interaction with climate change; more fully integrating the biological and ecological sciences, and the social, behavioral, and economic sciences with physical climate science; more comprehensively exploring the multiple space and timescales that characterize global change processes, including the role of natural climate variability and the importance of extremes; and investigating the complex, nonlinear behaviors in the Earth system and the tipping points that might be crossed as a result of global change.

Objective 1.2 describes the scientific advances needed to support effective and sustainable management of the risks of global change, according to the evolving priorities emerging from dialogue between the global change science community and the stakeholders and decision makers of broader society. Key elements include understanding potential vulnerabilities of natural and human systems in the face of global change; understanding essential elements of societal structure, governance, and human behavior necessary to know about human responses to change; applying fundamental scientific knowledge about the Earth system to support the development of adaptation and mitigation strategies for specific places, systems, and sectors, as well as for global-scale threats; and developing the scientific tools and methods needed to iteratively manage global change risks through these adaptation and mitigation responses.

The deeper understanding that is the aim of Objectives 1.1 and 1.2 will only be achieved by integrating observations of all essential Earth system components and processes, as discussed under Objective 1.3. Such integration is essential for developing theories and explanations of the causes and consequences of global change. These theoretical advances must in turn be captured and tested in integrated modeling systems for further advancement of fundamental scientific understanding, and for decision support, as described under Objective 1.4. Finally, success in all of these areas will need to build on continuing advances in information management and data sharing to aid scientific progress and to communicate with and inform society, as discussed under Objective 1.5.

Objective 1.1: Earth System Understanding

Advance fundamental understanding of the physical, chemical, biological, and human components of the Earth system, and the interactions among them, to improve knowledge of the causes and consequences of global change

Over the past two decades, research sponsored by USGCRP agencies has been critical in advancing the understanding of key aspects of global change science. These advances in knowledge of the components of the Earth system, gained from investment in observations, modeling, and fundamental theoretical research, have led to a growing appreciation for the complexity and interconnectedness of these components, the significant role that human activities play in global climate change, and the current and potential future rate, magnitude, and impacts of further change (see **Introduction**). Building on this history of success, the Program faces the challenge of continuing to develop the knowledge base required to help society respond to global change.

The seemingly disparate elements of Earth system science (**Box 9**) are in reality all connected across multiple dimensions and pathways. Similarly, global change has multiple linked and nested dimensions, including climate change; land-use and land-cover change; modification of the carbon, nitrogen, phosphorous, and sulfur cycles; pollution; loss of biodiversity and ecosystem functions and services; alteration of hydrologic systems; and human population dynamics, including growth, migration, and demographic shifts. To advance scientific understanding of the changing Earth system, the Program must consider many of these elements and their interdependencies as parts of one integrated research effort.

Some of the most important and challenging areas of future study will be located at the dynamic interfaces between components and processes—the ways in which one part of the Earth system influences the others. There are critical scientific issues that USGCRP and its member agencies cannot address comprehensively without adopting this systems perspective, such as risks to infrastructure, energy supply, food, water resources, and ecosystems, as well as how human behavior at multiple scales feeds back to influence the rate and nature of the change.

Box 9. Examples of Global Change in the Earth System and Related Processes
(intended to be illustrative rather than comprehensive). Equally crucial are the interactions among components.

Climate variability and change:

- Natural climate variability, including multiple space and times cales, deep-time events
- Cloud and aerosol processes and cloud-aerosol interactions
- Climate change impacts on ocean-atmosphere modes of variability
- Ocean dynamics, including regional variability
- Climate change effects on the hydrologic cycle, especially extreme events (storms, droughts, floods) and vice versa
- Changes in temperature extremes
- Cryospheric dynamics: ice sheets, ice caps, sea ice, glaciers, permafrost
- Sea-level rise and variability
- Feedbacks leading to abrupt change

Alteration of ecosystem structure and processes and land-use change:

- Urban systems and the built environment
- Development and urban encroachment
- Sustainability of agricultural ecosystems
- Fisheries dynamics and management strategies
- Tradeoffs between energy and food security
- Ecosystem sensitivity and resiliency
- Genomic resources of terrestrial and aquatic ecosystems
- Biodiversity, ecosystem resilience, and impacts of biological extinctions on ecosystem functions and services
- Economic value of ecosystem goods and services
- Conservation priorities for species and ecosystems
- Species abundance, range change, and invasive species

Demographic and socioeconomic trends in human society that drive global change:

- How human actions interact with global change over spatial, temporal, and organizational scales
- Population growth and migration
- Technological change
- Human consumption and production patterns
- Socio-political changes
- Public understanding of global change, risk perception, and communication of risk

Human outcomes and actions in response to global change:

- Vulnerability (exposure, sensitivity, adaptive capacity) of human and natural systems
- Management options that reduce greenhouse gas emissions and/or climate change impacts
- Human health and vulnerable populations
- Decision making under uncertainty
- Compensatory reactions to mitigation and adaptation
- Assessment of mitigation and adaptation options

Alteration of biogeochemical cycles:

- Ocean acidification and marine life cycles
- Carbon cycles; sources and sinks
- Nutrient cycles (e.g., nitrogen, iron, phosphorus)
- Changing atmospheric composition
- Nutrient imbalances, biogeochemical cycle interactions, and limitations
- Global resource extraction

Alteration of hydrologic systems:

- Groundwater resources, depletion, and pollution.
- Water supply, quality, and security
- Infrastructure changes (irrigation, water extraction, interbasin transfer, stormwater management, flood control)
- Changing recurrence probabilities for extreme events (floods, intense rainfall, drought)
- Coastal wetlands

USGCRP research must continue to deepen the understanding of individual natural and human Earth system components and processes and address the many critical research gaps that remain, particularly:

- The interactions and degree of interconnectedness between climate change and other critical elements of global change

- The fuller integration of the biological, biogeochemical, and ecological sciences with climate science

- The fuller integration of the social, behavioral, and economic sciences with climate science

- The coupling of multiple spatial and temporal scales, including the role of natural climate variability and the importance of extreme weather and climate events

- The complex Earth system behaviors that emerge from the mentioned component, process, and scale interactions

Pursuit of integrative research topics such as these will foster the development of a new cadre of researchers who are adept at working across disciplines and scales and able to deal with Earth system complexity in the development of responses to global change.

Box 10. Ocean Acidification

Food from the ocean is the primary source of protein for more than one billion people worldwide. Many jobs and economies in the United States and around the world depend on sustaining healthy fisheries. This task, already difficult in a world with a rapidly growing population, is made more complicated because of changes to the ocean resulting from fossil fuel combustion and the release of large additional amounts of carbon dioxide into the atmosphere (see also **Box 38**). The ocean absorbs a large fraction of this excess carbon dioxide, gradually increasing the acidity of its waters. If carbon dioxide emissions continue to grow at the present rate, it is estimated that by the end of this century, the ocean's surface waters will be about one and a half times more acidic than they were at the beginning of the Industrial Revolution in the mid-1800s. Scientists estimate that this ocean acidity level would be the highest in more than 20 million years. Moreover, paleoceanographic studies show that acidification of oceans during past geologic periods had severe consequences for carbonate-forming, or shell-bearing, organisms.

The increased acidity is affecting marine species to varying degrees. Laboratory studies demonstrate that ocean acidification is affecting the growth and lifespan of carbonate shell-forming organisms such as many plankton, mollusks, crustaceans, sea urchins, and corals. In addition, ocean acidification could affect these organisms in other ways, including shifting species distributions, reducing biodiversity, and increasing susceptibility to other stressors. Because these organisms form the base of the ocean's food web, these changes may affect fisheries worldwide.

USGCRP agencies are developing and deploying new ways to monitor ocean acidification. They are also supporting new research programs to understand the effects of ocean acidification on, for example, key organisms in the marine food web and the ecosystems they support, on coral reefs, and on the extent to which species can acclimate and adapt to ocean acidification.

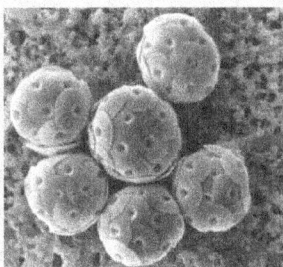 

Figure: Microscopic ocean phytoplankton grown in laboratory conditions with carbon dioxide levels that reflect present (left) and predicted future (2x present) atmospheric concentration (right). In the right figure, the armored plates (liths) of the phytoplankton have partially dissolved. Image courtesy of Ulf Riebesell.

Climate Change and Global Change

The Global Change Research Act of 1990 embraces an expansive definition of global change. Working within this definition, the Program has broadened its range of emphasis over time, from a primary focus on climate science toward a deeper integration of other Earth system science disciplines. One example is the long-standing research area of land-use and land cover change as both a driver of, and co-stressor with, climate change. This Strategic Plan continues along this trajectory to consider the complex, system-oriented phenomena that create global change more holistically. This will require fostering improved understanding, not only of the dynamical interactions among atmosphere, ocean, land, and ice, but also of the interactions between these climate system processes and other key dimensions of global change, such as ecosystem dynamics, key biogeochemical cycles **(Box 10)**, and human alteration of the water cycle**.**

This broader view is needed for effective responses to global change because such decisions rarely involve climate change in isolation. For many systems and sectors, particularly at local scales and in the near-term, climate change is not the only important stressor. For example, land clearing, urbanization and changes in transportation systems, and unsustainable agricultural practices, like poor irrigation management and overgrazing, are often the dominant drivers of ecosystem degradation, biodiversity loss, and the decline of water availability and quality. Climate change is likely to exacerbate many of the risks associated with these stressors, by further taxing the already compromised resilience of natural systems, and reducing the choices open to individuals, families, and policy makers.

Ultimately, the key science questions that address these and related issues can only be answered within a program of global change research that is broader than in the past—a program that moves closer to the vision put forward in its original founding legislation. The following subsections discuss in greater detail some of the most critical imperatives and substantive challenges the Program faces. The new and expanded knowledge base described therein threads throughout the remaining objectives of Advance Science and the remaining goals of this Strategic Plan.

Integration of the Biological Sciences

Greater integration of the biological sciences, including but not limited to the biogeochemical and ecological sciences, with the study of the physical climate system will be essential for a full realization of the Program goals and objectives. In the broadest sense, global change research includes the range of interactions between the biosphere and climate dynamics, from the exchange of carbon dioxide among different terrestrial and oceanic reservoirs, to the cycling of water, to the impacts of the biosphere on the radiative properties of the Earth's surface and atmosphere (see **Box 38**). The research must encompass the impacts of global change on all life on Earth and how those impacts may relate back to global change.

Improved integration is needed across multiple aspects and levels of the biological sciences. Processes at the population, species, community, and ecosystem levels are all critical for understanding the causes and consequences of global change. For example, a number of important ecosystem services (e.g., crop pollination) can only be understood through population- and community-level studies. Gaps remain in critical areas ranging from Earth system tipping points to the decisions humans make on sustaining and managing natural systems under a changing climate and other global change pressures (**Boxes 10 and 11**).

An integrated suite of observations that span the physical climate system and the biosphere, coupled with integrated models that capture the important intersections between life on Earth and the physical Earth system can advance integrated Earth system science and the knowledge base for managing risk. The USGCRP agencies currently carry out and sponsor a variety of research activities in many of these areas. The challenge for the Program in the next decade is better coordination of these activities with each other and with the Program's climate change research portfolio to advance integrated Earth system science and provide the new knowledge and knowledge syntheses required to inform decisions about managing the risks of global change.

Box 11. Species' Ranges Shift in Response to Global Change

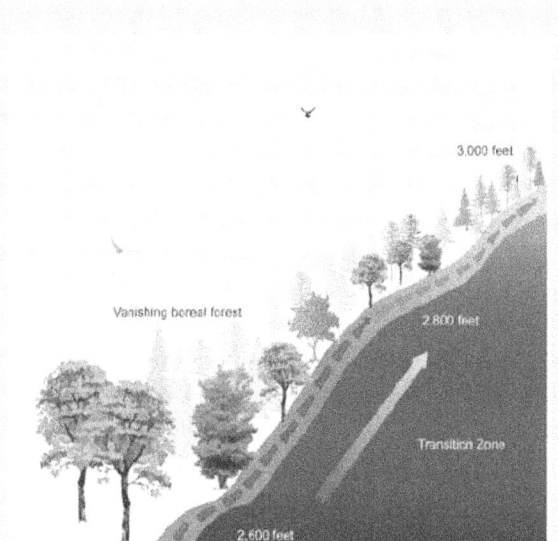

3,000 feet

Vanishing boreal forest

2,800 feet

Transition Zone

2,600 feet

Figure: As climate warms, hardwood trees out-compete evergreen trees that are adapted to colder conditions. Global change is resulting in major changes in the types of forests that will be most prevalent in different regions of the United States. Some common forests types are expected to expand, such as oak-hickory, while others, like maple-beech-birch, are expected to contract, or eventually disappear from the United States altogether. Industries, such as maple sugaring and tourism in the Northeast, would be strongly affected by these shifts.[7]

When the outside temperature gets too cold or too hot, humans can add or shed clothing, insulate their houses, and change thermostat settings. Other species do not have those options. Many plant and animal species have shifted their habitats poleward and upward in elevation in response to climate changes. By doing so, species may no longer have the resources essential for them to flourish and to provide ecosystem services. For example, species of birds and butterflies needed for agricultural pollination in a region might no longer be in that area, and as the ranges of species that carry human diseases change, disease risks to humans also may shift.

As climate change and other aspects of global change drive changes in species' ranges, entire ecosystems will be disrupted. Each species will shift according to its sensitivity to climate change, its mobility, its lifespan, and the availability of essential resources. Shifting also will depend on whether migratory pathways are blocked by development and habitat fragmentation (**Box 32**). In general, many existing ecosystems will be broken up and new ones formed.

USGCRP research is addressing the need for improved understanding of the rates and consequences of shifts in species' ranges through new, more comprehensive observations. By bringing together multiple data sources of species occurrence (collected by scientists, local and national governments, and citizen scientists), and incorporating these data into models of ecosystem and climate functioning, scientists can help predict important shifts for agriculture and forestry, assist in the strengthening of protected areas, and better respond to outbreaks of invasive species.

---

7. Beckage et al, 2008. A Rapid Upward Shift of a Forest Ecotone During 40 Years of Warming in the Green Mountains of Vermont. Proceedings of the National Academy of Sciences 2008, 105(11), p. 4197-4202. Schematic adapted from J. Abundis.

Integration of the Social, Behavioral, and Economic Sciences

A number of recent reports have argued that many of the critical questions related to understanding and responding to global change cannot be adequately addressed without substantial contributions from the social, behavioral, and economic sciences. For example, population dynamics, natural resource consumption patterns, economic development, governance, and the development and adoption of new technologies underlie the human drivers of global change. Global change will affect death and migration rates, consumption of energy and other resources, and attitudes about the adoption of new technologies. At the same time, mitigation and adaptation activities are likely to interact with the Earth system in complex ways.

Similarly, the cognitive basis for decision making governs individual and societal responses to global change, and these actions occur within, and are constrained by, institutions, social networks, and political, economic, and cultural contexts. These, in turn, interact with public understanding of science and technology, as well as risk perception and communication. Advances in technology have the power to promote public engagement with science and harness public participation in research.

All of these issues, and many others, will be important for USGCRP over the next decade and necessitate a coordinated response. The Program will take on the challenge of fostering and integrating the contributions of economists, geographers, anthropologists, cognitive scientists, sociologists, political scientists, urban planners, public health researchers, and other experts with ongoing and planned new research activities in the physical, chemical, and biological sciences (see, e.g., **Box 12**).

Meeting this challenge requires expanding the engagement of these disciplines in global change science to achieve a deeper understanding of the vulnerabilities and responses to global change. Part of the solution will be to use the coordination mechanisms of the Program to enhance dialogue and collaboration between these communities. Another part will be to leverage the expertise in agencies, or parts of agencies, that have not traditionally been part of USGCRP. Specific recommendations for improving integration of social, behavioral, and economic sciences for supporting adaptation and mitigation decisions, developing an integrated observational capability, developing next generation integrated models, and advancing information management and sharing are discussed under subsequent Advance Science objectives. In addition, the engagement, decision support, and assessment activities of the Program are expected to open fruitful new avenues for this inquiry. For example, the Program will be able to harness the enhanced capacity in social, behavioral, and economic sciences that will be developed and sustained under the auspices of the National Climate Assessment (NCA, refer to Goal 3).

Box 12. Climate Change and Human Health

The impacts of disease as varied as heart disease, asthma, Lyme disease, and Salmonella infections rise and fall based on changes in weather and climate. As the Nation's climate changes, vulnerable people and communities will be at risk of more frequent or severe health problems. In addition to deaths and illnesses related to increasing heat and other weather extremes, people will be affected by changes in water supplies and contaminants, food quality, and other ecosystem effects. For example, changes in climate are expected to change habitat suitability for *Ixodes scapularis*, the tick vector of Lyme disease.

The decisions and strategies used to reduce greenhouse gases and protect communities from climate effects also have important health implications. For example, reducing combustion of fossil fuels as a means of reducing carbon dioxide levels may lower the levels of many harmful air pollutants, like soot. And adaptation measures such as higher capacity storm water management systems may provide the opportunity to reduce health risks from combined sewer overflow events.

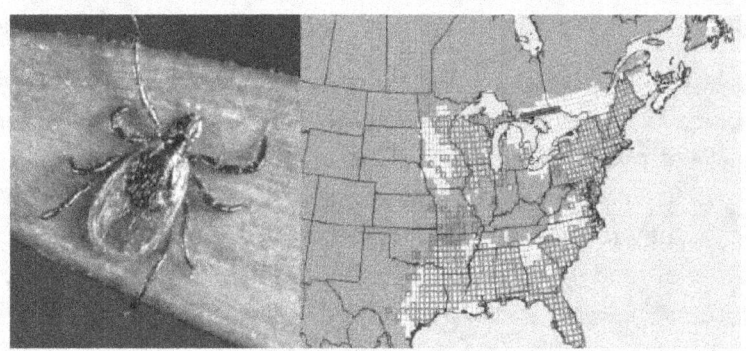

Figure: (left) An Ixodes tick vector of Lyme Disease; (right): Distribution of climate-based habitat suitability for Ixodes scapularis. Image courtesy of Jim Gathany/CDC.

USGCRP will help meet the complex challenges of climate change and human health by building the integrated knowledge base needed to understand, predict, respond, and adapt to these changes. USGCRP provides coordination of basic climate and health research, monitoring and health surveillance, vulnerability and risk assessments, and communication, education, and engagement efforts across the Federal government, in partnership with organizations in the United States and around the world.

A new USGCRP coordination effort is the Monitoring, Early Warning, Data Integration and Surveillance (MEDS) online tool. This electronic information portal is intended to help public health professionals, researchers, and other users identify and use relevant climate and health datasets in their region of interest. MEDS, which will launch in early 2012, captures critical characteristics of the datasets, including time and geographic scales, health outcomes, and data resolution.

Figure: On Tuvalu, a low-lying island in the Pacific, frequent floods, due to rising sea levels, expose people to contaminated water. Image courtesy of Jocelyn Carlin/Panos Pictures.

Multiple Space and Time Scales, Natural Variability, and Extremes

While global change can refer to change at the scale of the entire Earth system, it can also refer to local changes happening in many places around the world. In aggregate, these local changes can have global consequences. Local impacts of long-term global change are often indirect and realized through complex interactions with phenomena occurring over a wide range of space and time scales. Over the next decade, the Program will need to foster greater scientific progress on fundamental questions related to the effects of Earth system processes and behaviors at one scale on those at another, the potential for processes in one place to affect other regions around the world, and the implications of these scale interactions for the understanding of, and responses to, global change.

Earth's climate varies naturally on timescales of seasons to decades, or longer, as a result of dynamic interactions between the atmosphere and the ocean. The best-known example is the El Niño Southern Oscillation phenomenon, which causes significant year-to-year variations in temperature and rainfall in many different regions around the world, notably the western U.S. **(Box 13)**. Other longer-term patterns, such as the Pacific Decadal Oscillation, the Northern and Southern Annular Modes, the North Atlantic Oscillation, and the Atlantic Multidecadal Oscillation, have similarly important regional impacts on agriculture, fisheries, transportation, and energy supply and demand.

Understanding how these natural oscillations control yearly and decadal variations in regional climate worldwide, as well as how they may change in the future as a result of global climate change, is essential for informing decisions in agriculture, water resources, disaster management, and many other societally critical sectors. In addition, other Earth system processes and external forcings, such as volcanic, solar, and orbital variations, also drive climate system variability and interact in complex ways with the mentioned internal ocean-atmosphere oscillations and human-caused climate change. Ongoing and new observations, as well as improved modeling, of the Earth's energy budget – at the top of the atmosphere, in melting ice, atmospheric convection, and other transformations of water, and in the ocean – will be crucial for understanding variability in the climate system.

On shorter timescales, weather and climate extremes such as hurricanes, tornadoes, torrential downpours, heat waves, and droughts affect all sectors of the economy and the environment, impacting people where they live, work, and grow their food. Critical research questions for the Program in the next decade relate to whether such extremes are changing in intensity, duration, frequency, timing, and spatial extent as a result of climate change, and the potential for the occurrence of unprecedented extremes.

The impacts of extremes on society are a strong function of local vulnerability, determined to a large extent by factors such as settlement patterns, governance, socioeconomic development, and the consumption of ecosystem services. Other kinds of Earth system extremes, such as harmful algal blooms, wildfires, air pollution episodes, and disease outbreaks, also have crucial environmental and societal implications, and often interact with weather and climate extremes. All of these dimensions will require increased attention in the Program over the next decade.

Box 13. El Niño Southern Oscillation (ENSO)

The El Niño Southern Oscillation (ENSO) climate phenomenon can dramatically affect weather over much of the United States, as well as over large swaths of South America. ENSO is a result of a coupling of the ocean and the atmosphere. The "warm phase", El Niño, is characterized by a shift of warm water from its normal position in the western Pacific to the eastern Pacific off Peru. The "cold phase," La Niña, is characterized by colder waters in the equatorial Pacific. In recent years, partnerships between USGCRP agencies have resulted in improving scientific understanding, which has made possible the prediction of ENSO up to a year or more in advance in some cases. This prediction requires integration of long-term, sustained satellite observations and *in situ* (in place) ocean measurements (such as an array of buoys designed to monitor ENSO) with theoretical advances in atmospheric and oceanic dynamics and sophisticated computer modeling. These increased predictive capabilities have translated directly into large societal benefits – from farmers being able to plan for the major shifts in rainfall, to governments shifting resources to cope with flooding or altered energy demand in response to unusually hot or cold weather.

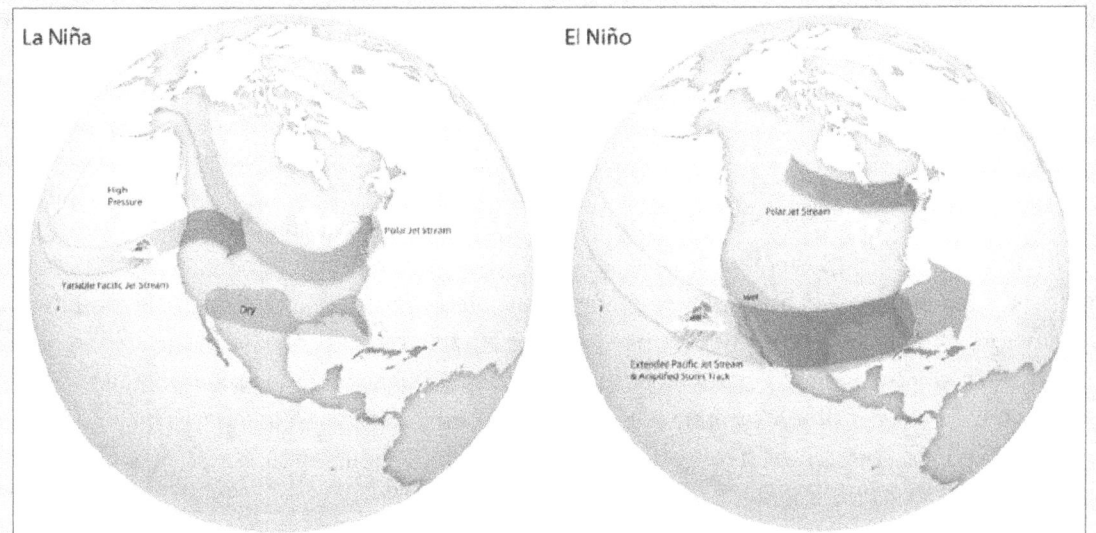

Figure: Improved understanding of ENSO (which can last from 6 -18 months and occurs approximately every 3-7 years) has allowed for prediction of effects on the U.S. up to a year in advance. In El Niño phases, the Pacific Jet Stream brings increased rain to the southern tier of the U.S., and warm weather to the northern tier. In contrast, La Niña results in drier weather in the south, warmer than normal winter temperatures in the southeast, and cooler than normal temperatures in the northwest. Image courtesy of NOAA.

Climate science continues to identify other natural patterns of variability in the climate system, occurring over timescales from seasons to decades, which have a similarly strong influence on weather in the U.S. and worldwide. Recently recognized climate patterns include the Arctic Oscillation that affects U.S. weather and Arctic sea ice (**Box 17**), the Pacific Decadal Oscillation that affects Pacific fisheries, and the Atlantic Meridional Oscillation that affects the frequency of Atlantic hurricanes and U.S. rainfall and air temperatures. Grasping climate system variations can be likened to weaving a symphony together from the disparate strands of individual melodies. Taken together, they drive much of the observed variability in the weather that's experienced locally. Over the next decade, the USGCRP agencies must not only continue to support the necessary observing assets to maintain progress toward improved predictions for these natural cycles, but also to document and understand how ENSO and other patterns of variability will shift in both time (the frequency and intensity of the cycles) and space (where they are located regionally) as climate changes.

Addressing these and related questions will call for a focus on finer spatial and temporal resolution in observations and modeling to link, for example, climate system processes with the dynamics of ecosystems and human communities. It will also require integrating the aggregate effects of small-scale, short-term processes and behaviors (both human and natural) into the understanding of Earth system behaviors at the global scale. Finally, it will entail a focus, not just on long-term averages, but on the effects of global change on much shorter timescale phenomena such as the extremes discussed previously. These imperatives will place particularly challenging demands on the observational, modeling, and data management capabilities of the Program.

Complexity, Thresholds, and Tipping Points

Understanding global change is difficult because the Earth system is complex, with behavior that emerges as a result of many interactions on multiple scales among the atmosphere, ocean, ice sheets, land surface, and the biosphere. People add to this complexity because they are a part of the Earth system, and play a unique role in it. They not only influence but are influenced by Earth system changes. They can also consciously choose how to respond to these changes while considering and observing the implications of their response.

This multiplicity of interconnections among different Earth system components, and among processes occurring at different scales, can lead to changes that are difficult to observe, measure, monitor, or model as they are starting to occur. Thus, anticipating these changes and responding effectively are more challenging. Some system-wide changes can appear relatively slowly, on pace with changes in interacting components, such as land-use change associated with population growth. Some, however, can emerge abruptly, with little prior warning, such as a potential mass release to the atmosphere of methane stored in ocean sediments or Arctic permafrost. Such behavior results when conditions exceed a critical threshold in environmental stability – a tipping point – thereby leading to a major alteration of the system in a short period of time. These shifts often are also effectively irreversible on anything other than very long timescales.

There is clear evidence that Earth's climate is capable of large and rapid shifts, with cascading effects through natural systems documented in the records of ice cores, tree rings, and lake and ocean sediments. Over the last 10,000 years, sources of climate variability like oscillations in the atmosphere-ocean system and volcanic eruptions have created severe droughts and other regional climate events. These events were characterized by abrupt onset and sustained duration, often with deleterious effects on human settlements and civilizations.

What makes the human-driven global changes happening in the 21st century uniquely significant are the speed and potential magnitude of change on a planet now populated by billions of people. Research on the properties of complex systems suggests that large, abrupt changes in the Earth system will become increasingly likely with increasing disturbance. Earth may approach new and as yet unidentified tipping points in its biological systems, the biogeochemical cycles that help regulate the concentrations of greenhouse gases in the atmosphere, ocean circulation patterns, and ice sheet stability. Such changes could occur so rapidly that they would challenge the ability of human and natural systems to adapt. The current scientific understanding must be improved significantly before these risks can be comprehensively assessed and used to inform risk management decisions and strategies.

In response to this need, USGCRP will place a high priority on research to understand rates, processes, mechanisms, and consequences of global change and the complex, nonlinear climatic, ecological, and social system dynamics leading to abrupt changes, thresholds, and tipping points. Understanding of past changes in temperature, precipitation, ocean chemistry, sea level, and sensitivity to changes in atmospheric carbon dioxide levels gained from studying the paleoclimatic record will play a critical role in this research (**Box 41**). The long time series data provided by paleoclimatic records are invaluable for improving understanding of natural variability on decadal and longer timescales, and the sampling of climatic conditions very different from the past century or two of direct climate measurements provides crucial tests of model performance. In addition, the Program will need to foster significant advances in the understanding of the potential unintended consequences of actions taken in response to global change, as such actions themselves have the potential to upset natural balances in significant and potentially unexpected ways.

Objective 1.2: Science for Adaptation and Mitigation

Advance understanding of the vulnerability and resilience of integrated human-natural systems and enhance the usability of scientific knowledge in supporting responses to global change

The strategy for advancing USGCRP science in the next decade has a dual aim. The first, as discussed under Objective 1.1, is to achieve a deeper, more fundamental understanding of the integrated Earth system – its natural and human components and their interaction. The second, discussed here, is to advance use-inspired science to assess vulnerabilities to global change, understand the societal and ecological characteristics that confer resilience in the face of these changes, and support the adaptation and mitigation responses to the risks these changes pose.

In this context, "use-inspired" refers to science that is needed to improve fundamental understanding in areas important to people and society. Use-inspired research may be curiosity driven but it is anchored by a consideration of the importance of a particular scientific question as a function of its societal relevance. The knowledge and insights emerging from such research are intended to be applied toward the identification and evaluation of options to reduce the risks of global change. To accomplish this objective, the Program will need to fully leverage and support the varied capabilities and missions of its Federal agency members, as well as engage more deeply with other communities well versed in vulnerability and risk management, disaster management, public health, and national defense.

This objective, of advancing the science essential to understand and manage the risks of global change, is embedded within the broader concept of sustainability, which considers how to meet society's current needs without compromising those of future generations or Earth's essential life support systems. USGCRP research relates to sustainability in two specific ways: first, because of the significant overlap between the knowledge base and practices of sustainable environmental and natural resource management and those expected to be useful for adaptation and mitigation; second, because of the potential for sustainability co-benefits of well-chosen adaptation and mitigation strategies.

Systematic identification and characterization of the most urgent vulnerabilities and the biggest risks faced from global change, so as to respond effectively and sustainably, are societal challenges. Scientific discovery and societal concern have complementary roles: science identifies emerging problems (e.g., the ozone hole or human-caused climate change), analyzes the feasibility of response options, proposes new options, and monitors to track progress; society communicates its requirements and the values that guide where and how urgently to respond and the preferred set of responses. Both evolve together in an iterative and collaborative dialogue.

In the next decade, USGCRP will embody this dialogue by providing the scientific foundation for global change risk management in the areas of greatest societal need, as defined and guided by the strategic priorities of decision makers and stakeholders. The Program will engage with them through its communication, assessment, and decision support efforts described under Goals 2, 3, and 4. Major themes of this effort include:

- Identifying and understanding key environmental and societal vulnerabilities to global change over a range of space and time scales

- Developing a knowledge base to support regional and sectoral responses to global change

- Developing a knowledge base to support responses to global-scale threats

- Creating and applying the tools and approaches needed to iteratively manage the risks of global change

Broadly, this suite of focus areas encompasses both research *for* and *on* decision support. It includes research to develop knowledge about vulnerable systems, potential impacts, and response options, as well as knowledge about decision making processes themselves to help construct effective decision frameworks, identify information needs, and illuminate barriers.

Understanding Vulnerability to Global Change

The concept of vulnerability refers to the degree to which a system is susceptible to, and unable to cope with, adverse impacts of global change. Along with its subconcepts of exposure, sensitivity, and adaptive capacity, vulnerability provides a major thread linking science, society, and decision making about responses to global change. It helps focus scientific research around key societal concerns and provides a framework for identifying the sectors, regions, resources, and populations that are most at risk from the impacts of global change. It also aligns strongly with foundational concepts of environmental management, such as risk assessment and benefit-cost analysis, thereby providing a bridge between scientists and the managers who will be in the front lines of adaptation and mitigation actions.

The interdependence of Earth system components and processes, as described in Objective 1.1, dictates that vulnerability assessment will be most effective when it focuses on the larger system within which a particular ecosystem, human community, or socioeconomic sector is embedded. In this context, assessment of coupled human-environment systems will be a major focus for USGCRP in the next decade. For example, urban areas, coastal settlements, and agricultural systems concentrate people, infrastructure, and economic assets, and therefore introduce the potential for vulnerability to shifts in the environment that surrounds, connects, and supports them—shifts that result from natural variability, longer-term global change trends, or a combination of the two.

Key natural resources and socioeconomic sectors, such as water, energy, agriculture, transportation, fisheries, forestry, health, and military operations and infrastructure, are strongly connected to the environment, and thus vulnerable to natural variability and global change. They are also strongly connected to each other. For example, water supply systems use large amounts of energy (e.g., for treatment and delivery) while, simultaneously, energy systems use large amounts of water (e.g., for hydropower and cooling). Both are expected to be under pressure from increasing demand in the future, and both will be affected by aspects of global change such as a changing climate. Changes in energy policy and production that might be undertaken to mitigate human-caused climate change could also have significant consequences for water availability and quality. Research about human behavior that influences consumption and production, especially social networks and the governance of resources, would also contribute significantly to understanding vulnerability in these sectors. Understanding the interconnections and competition among resource sectors such as water, food, and energy, and more broadly, the vulnerability of coupled human-environment systems, will help provide societally relevant frames for USGCRP research (**Box 14**).

Identification of differences in vulnerability across space and time is another key research theme going forward. For example, global change impacts are, and will continue to be, distributed unevenly across nations, communities, households, and individuals, creating differing levels of vulnerability, with important implications for adaptation and mitigation. Research into how individuals, families, businesses, and communities will experience sea-level rise, human health stressors, and varying precipitation patterns will contribute to understanding variations in vulnerability across space and time.

Box 14. Food Security, Energy Security, and Climate Change

Food, energy, and water are closely interconnected and their production both influences and is influenced by global change. Changing climatic conditions, including more frequent and intense storms and droughts, stress food production systems. Moreover, as more energy is being used to produce food, more of the agricultural production is being used to produce energy in the form of biofuels. While enhancing energy security and climate mitigation, biofuels from corn and soybeans compete directly with food crops. U.S. Department of Agriculture (USDA) predicted that in 2011, more corn would go to ethanol than to animal feed for the first time.[8] The large-scale increase in biofuel feedstocks also can compete with forests, natural grasslands, and private conservation lands with implications for the many ecosystem services they provide, and for net greenhouse gas emissions. These systems and others that produce biofuels can be balanced against the energy savings and potential greenhouse gas reductions of biofuels, as well as against the food demands of a growing population.

Greenhouse gas emissions are only one part of the complex interactions between food, energy, and climate. As climate changes challenge the ability to grow crops for food and energy, more irrigation and water management will be warranted. As precipitation patterns shift, available water for irrigating crops may decrease at the same time as there is greater demand for both growing and processing biofuel crops. More irrigation uses more water and more energy, which results in more greenhouse gas emissions. Greater water demands for food and energy production also compete with changing demands for this limited resource for domestic and industrial applications. The link among food, energy, water, and climate change is one example of the increasingly complex web of physical, biological, economic, and social systems in a rapidly developing and globalizing world.

Figure: (top) Industrial Biorefinery in York County, Nebraska. Image courtesy of DOE. (bottom) Crop irrigation. Image courtesy of USDA ARS.

Managers and policy makers will need to manage tradeoffs among food, energy, and water demands in a changing climate, while minimizing risks and unintended consequences of related decisions. To do so, they will need a deeper understanding of the ways in which use and production of these critical resources are interdependent, and how these interdependencies are affected by global change. Decisions that need to be made by farmers and land managers as well as national and international policy makers will benefit greatly from a synthesis of inputs from economists, social scientists, natural scientists, and modelers. Decision making also will call for improved understanding of decision processes, and how improved scientific information can support these decisions. USGCRP can address decision making needs through the coordination of social and natural sciences research across its member agencies. One example is interdisciplinary research into the environmental footprints of existing and proposed biofuels, which may lead to better decision making about fuel choices. Aided by USGCRP support of integrated observational systems, researchers and decision makers will be able to simultaneously track food, energy, and water production and use, as well as climate shifts and variability. Increasingly complex data will provide the foundation for informed decision making to maximize the benefits of the choices humans make about food, energy, and water resources in the face of global change.

8. USDA World Agricultural Outlook Board, 2011. *World Agricultural Supply and Demand Estimates* Report.

Similarly, as with human systems, the impacts of global change on natural systems are distributed unevenly across species, habitats, and ecosystems, with certain systems (e.g., coral reefs, tropical forests, wetlands and estuaries, and high-altitude habitats) being particularly vulnerable. The Program will aim to foster advances in research in these areas, as well as on related questions of interactions between ecological and societal impacts of global change. For example, exploration of the implications of global change for biodiversity is an important research need, as biodiversity is a crucial foundation for societal necessities such as food, fiber, and pharmaceuticals, as well as ecosystem services such as clean air, fresh water, and waste disposal.

The ultimate purpose of identifying and characterizing vulnerabilities is to support development and assessment of options to reduce and manage risk. The Program will create a knowledge base and evaluation capability for identifying critical global change vulnerabilities across a continuum of scales: from global, long-term threats to the stability of the whole Earth system to regional, near-term threats to particular ecosystems, human communities and populations, and socioeconomic sectors. Understanding the magnitude and rate of change, the entities impacted, and how their responses to change feed back into the Earth system, are vital research ends that span this scale continuum. Building from this understanding, the Program will be able to implement a robust research agenda for the two major and interlinked categories of global change responses—adaptation and mitigation—and in so doing advance the development of actionable knowledge to support decision making about effective adaptation and mitigation strategies.

Science to Support Regional and Sectoral Responses

A key Program need in the next decade is to foster new research on methods for quantifying, tracking, and, ultimately, enhancing the adaptive capacity of ecosystems, places, human communities, and socioeconomic sectors in the face of global change. For example, social and economic factors (e.g., economic status, age, gender, cultural or identity affiliation, and health) can significantly affect people's exposure to global change impacts, the degree to which these impacts affect them, and their capacity for adaptation to these effects. Understanding these factors is fundamental for addressing the equity issues associated with national and international policies aimed at mitigating global change and its impacts.

Incorporating learning from the social, behavioral, and economic sciences will be required to improve understanding of this differential adaptive capacity and to learn about the characteristics of resilient populations and communities. Systematically integrating outside scientific research and information products with local knowledge will be critical for identifying feasible and effective adaptation and mitigation options. In addition, the Program must foster research to develop metrics, indicators, and frameworks to enable the transfer of knowledge about response strategies across sectors and regions, as also discussed under Goal 3 of this Strategic Plan.

Furthermore, because adaptation and mitigation will likely provoke transformations of infrastructure and the built environment, both as drivers of global change and sources of vulnerability to impacts (e.g., the nexus of coastal transportation infrastructure, sea-level rise, and storm surge), it will be critical for the Program to build new partnerships with engineers, architects, and planners and their supporting Federal agencies (**Box 15**). Leveraging international partnerships will be essential for applying relevant experience and information in adaptation and mitigation from around the world to here in the United States and vice-versa.

Similarly, new knowledge about the resilience and adaptive capacity of populations, species, and ecosystems will be critical. For example, field studies indicate that ecosystems degraded by overharvesting, habitat destruction, pollution, and other stressors tend to have less resilience in the face of global change, thus necessitating more aggressive conservation efforts. The capacity for societal adaptation will depend, in part, on the aggregate impacts of global change on biodiversity and ecosystem services, such as clean water, flood protection, and food production.

In many cases, ecologists require significantly improved understanding of the detailed processes that lead from individual species to ecosystem functioning as a prerequisite for helping environmental and natural resource managers design and implement effective strategies for preserving and promoting natural ecological resilience to global change. For example, maintaining ecosystem integrity in the face of climate change will likely require restoration of disturbed ecosystems, but many fundamental questions of restoration ecology remain unanswered. Therefore, to aid in the overall effort to build a knowledge base for regional and sectoral responses to global change, the Program must coordinate and encourage focused research to understand the resilience and adaptive capacity of ecosystems, and the corresponding implications for people and society.

Box 15. Sea-Level Rise and Coastal Vulnerability

Sea-level rise directly affects the hundreds of millions of people worldwide that live in coastal regions. In addition to flooding homes, sea-level rise can increase coastal erosion, degrade wetlands, and make surface and ground water salty and unusable for irrigation or drinking water. Scientific measurements show that sea level has been rising steadily over the past century (see figure for the last two decades). This rise is due primarily to expansion of the ocean as it warms and melting of land ice (glaciers and ice sheets), with each of these factors making a roughly equal contribution to the current rate of sea-level rise. There also is a great deal of regional variation, which is due to ocean circulation patterns and geological and tectonic processes. As global temperatures continue to increase, scientists expect that melting of the Greenland and Antarctic ice sheets—which hold an additional 64 meters (210 feet) of sea level—will accelerate, becoming the largest contributor to sea-level rise.

Protecting vulnerable coastal communities from sea-level rise in the years ahead calls for a better understanding of the processes that influence sea level. This information can then be used to improve models that project the rates and patterns of sea-level rise under a range of global change scenarios. The measured rate of global sea-level rise over the past 20 years has been higher than those simulated by the models in the last Intergovernmental Panel on Climate Change (IPCC) assessment. This is due primarily to the current generation of models being unable to fully capture the processes that determine the melting of the Greenland and Antarctic ice sheets.

Over the next decade, USGCRP and its member agencies will help advance the models scientists and planners use to project future sea-level rise and coordinate research efforts to improve scientific understanding of natural

Figure: Aerial photo showing gradual barrier island erosion and subsequent flooding of facilities in coastal Lousiana. Rising sea levels are projected to increase coastal erosion, and the frequency and severity of damaging storm surges and flooding. Image courtesy of Tim Carruthers, Integration and Application Network, University of Maryland Center for Environmental Science (ian.umces.edu/imagelibrary/).

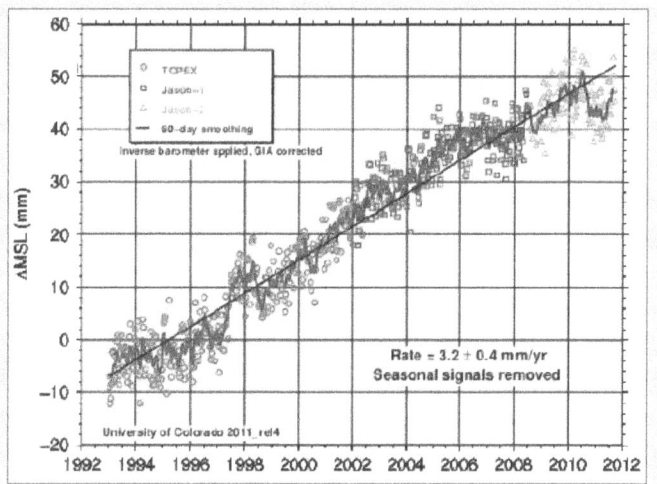

Figure: Global mean sea level time series. Documentation of this global change trend has been possible through a commitment within USGCRP to maintaining strong satellite observing systems and through partnerships among USGCRP member agencies and international partners. (http://sealevel.colorado.edu/content/2011rel4-global-mean-sea-level-time-series-seasonal-signals-removed). Image courtesy of the University of Colorado.

fluctuations in sea level and the mechanisms and rates by which ice sheets melt. The Program will also focus on linking improved scientific knowledge and modeling capability with a greater understanding of additional influential factors, including the social, economic, and ecosystem dynamics of coastal areas to better support decision making about adapting to the consequences of rising sea levels.

Science to Support Global-Scale Responses

USGCRP must enhance existing research, and foster new research, to support development of actions to reduce the global-scale risks associated with the different dimensions of global change, such as global warming, ocean acidification, global sea-level rise, and widespread loss of biodiversity. For example, the identification, development, implementation, and evaluation of effective greenhouse gas mitigation strategies require an integrated understanding of carbon storage in the Earth system, the human actions that lead to greenhouse gas emissions changes, and the risks of extreme consequences of greenhouse gas-induced global climate and carbon cycle change (see **Box 38**). To achieve this improved understanding, the Program must promote new forest, soil, agricultural, and ecosystem research that is fundamental to understanding carbon stocks, sequestration, and natural greenhouse gas fluxes. An improved understanding of how species interactions lead to healthy, functioning ecosystems is a prerequisite for understanding how restoration ecology can be applied to enhance carbon storage and hence greenhouse gas mitigation. Similarly, new research on ocean chemistry and circulation is needed to better quantify oceanic uptake of carbon dioxide. Broadly, the Program will need to develop the capability to comprehensively assess the potential of land, freshwater, and ocean ecosystems to increase net uptake of carbon dioxide and other greenhouse gases. In addition, the Program will need to foster improved understanding of the potential for simultaneously enhancing food production and reducing greenhouse gas emissions through improved agricultural practices and management strategies.

Progress in understanding the role of radiatively active gaseous and aerosol compounds with short atmospheric lifetimes compared to the major greenhouse gases will also be needed, as management and production of these species have the potential to either complement or confound mitigation responses (**Box 24**). Improved understanding of links between air quality and climate change will be essential for supporting the development of strategies that can limit the magnitude of climate change while improving air quality. An important aspect of this research that also links back to adaptation will be to characterize and quantify the contributions of urban areas to both local and global changes in climate, and develop and test approaches for affecting these contributions.

Making progress in the natural sciences to support mitigation efforts will also require the Program to foster advances in the social, behavioral, and economic sciences. Such advances are needed to improve understanding of human actions that lead to climate change and other global changes. For example, these advances are required to improve understanding of how individuals, families, businesses, and other institutions make choices about energy usage and technological change that lead to changes in emissions, and hence atmospheric composition, ocean chemistry, and climate. Understanding the costs and benefits of those choices and the social, behavioral, and institutional obstacles to adoption of new behaviors and technologies are critical inputs to decision making and the development of future scenarios.

More broadly, improving understanding of the many interactions between climate and energy, such as the interaction between renewable energy technologies and production, water usage, and climate-related impacts on water availability, among many other examples, will be a particularly important element of this research and a key dimension of exploring the interactions and trade-offs between mitigation and adaptation. In coordinating such research, USGCRP will leverage its partnership with the interagency Climate Change Technology Program (CCTP) whose purpose is to accelerate development, reduce the cost, and promote the deployment of new and advanced technologies and best practices that could avoid, reduce, capture, or store greenhouse gas emissions.[9] CCTP will need to inform USGCRP as new technologies are developed and implemented that affect future emissions trajectories. Similarly, USGCRP will need to inform CCTP regarding the potential global change impacts of and on the implementation of these new technologies.

Informing the pace and magnitude of adaptation and mitigation efforts requires improved understanding of the potential for crossing thresholds and tipping points in physical, ecological, and social systems. To gain this understanding, USGCRP should promote research on catastrophic consequences of rapid global change, such as extreme global warming, collapse of major ice sheets, massive biodiversity losses, global natural resource collapse, and destruction of major infrastructure such as dams, seawalls, and transportation systems. This research will need to leverage fundamental scientific understanding gained through the Program's research efforts in key Earth system processes, such as cloud microphysics, stratospheric dynamics and chemistry, biological productivity in the oceans, and biophysical modulation of surface albedo.

Improved understanding in the area of potential catastrophic consequences would also be helpful should there be a desire to develop the capacity to assess the feasibility, effectiveness, and unintended consequences of proposed strategies for deliberate, large-scale modification of Earth's environment, such as solar radiation management or capture of carbon dioxide, intended to partially offset the harmful consequences of greenhouse gas-induced climate change.

Tools and Approaches for Iterative Risk Management

Effective and sustainable management of the long-term risks from global change must be iterative. This holds across the spectrum of regional, sectoral, and global adaptation and mitigation actions. An iterative process of research, decision support, monitoring, evaluation, and learning can reduce risk and promote adaptive management in the context of global change. Over the next decade, USGCRP will step up its efforts to contribute to the development and enhancement of tools and approaches essential to realizing this process, including decision support frameworks, scenarios, valuation methodologies, and indicators. The aspirational goal is the eventual institutionalization of a national learning process in coping with global change.

A broad challenge for USGCRP will be to help define best practices for transforming new scientific knowledge into actionable information. This information will be needed to support the adaptation and mitigation priorities that will flow from the decision maker and stakeholder engagement activities of the Program. A large body of literature about how decisions are made, and how innovations and new concepts are diffused, makes clear that scientific knowledge is only one part of a much broader process. Information may be scientifically relevant without being decision relevant (**Box 16**).

The range of potentially useful decision support frameworks and perspectives is large. This encompasses approaches that rely on accurate predictions, methods to identify solutions that are robust in the face of deep uncertainty about the future, and precautionary approaches that set hard limits for acceptable consequences. Identifying the right portfolio of risk management options for a particular region, sector,

---

9. For more information, visit http://climatetechnology.gov/.

or type of global change impact will require decision support frameworks appropriate for the characteristics of the given problem and tailored to the decision context of the specific stakeholders involved.

To maximize relevance for adaptation and mitigation decision making, the Program will strive to foster science that is coherent and meaningful within specific decision contexts, integrates across disciplines, and engages stakeholders as participants. Research that incorporates these considerations will be particularly important in the following areas:

- Developing models and tools to assess the environmental, social, human health, and economic outcomes of alternative adaptation and mitigation options

- Developing scenarios of possible global change impacts, including extremes and high-consequence events

- Identifying social and ecological thresholds that help define limits to adaptation and the options for mitigation

- Characterizing uncertainties for the many decisions necessary to respond to human-driven global change, particularly at the local scale (as they are for most of the important policy decisions faced by society)

The Program will embed these and related considerations in its research design and delivery of global change assessments and services to inform decision making about responding to global change. In addition, the Program will seize the opportunity to sponsor vital social sciences research that evaluates the uptake of USGCRP research into adaptation and mitigation decisions and its effectiveness in informing outcomes. Strong partnerships with regulatory agencies, collaborative science and applications initiatives at the regional level, and international efforts will be essential for both enhancing Program capacity and ensuring the relevance of its research activities.

Scenario development and application will be a critical input to such decision support frameworks, as discussed in Objective 1.4. Improving methods and the knowledge base for developing and discovering climate, demographic, socioeconomic, and technological scenarios meaningful in particular decision contexts will require significant and sustained attention from the Program. While models will be essential tools of scenario development, there is room for considerable expansion of scenario development efforts based on historical and paleoclimate data, particularly in the context of assessing vulnerability to rare and potentially damaging extremes.

The development of a new generation of environmental management tools and approaches will be a key frontier in supporting progress toward responding effectively to global change. Because of the long time horizons, the varied levels of scientific uncertainties regarding how human-caused change will impact human and natural systems, and the highly distributed impacts across systems and sectors, including those difficult to value economically, global change poses unique challenges for the foundational tools and approaches of environmental management, such as risk assessment and benefit-cost analysis. Across all categories of global change response strategies, advances in methods for estimating the damages associated with regional and sectoral impacts are required for informed analyses of the benefits of adaptation and mitigation efforts. The Program will therefore also explore new frameworks for assessing risks and benefits that account for these challenges and allow policy makers to better understand the impacts, co- benefits, and potential unintended consequences of adaptation and mitigation options.

One of the most important conceptual and practical challenges to developing robust iterative approaches is the lack of understanding about which variables need to be monitored and what metrics of risk are most useful to decision makers. In the same way that economic decisions are based upon a broad and carefully developed set of indicators (e.g., gross domestic product, unemployment), global change-related decisions should be informed by a broadly recognized set of indicators that track changing environmental conditions, vulnerability, and adaptive capacity at local to international scales. Development of such metrics and indicators will be essential for supporting iterative management of global change risks, as well as to transfer learning about vulnerabilities and response strategies across sectors and regions.

Broad-based, coordinated planning efforts among the relevant research and user communities will be needed to identify the highest priorities for data collection, data integration, and indicator development. For example, the potential exists for increased use of remote sensing (validated against *in situ* measurements) to develop indicators of change simultaneously over large areas. Improvements in this area have the potential to transform monitoring of the variations in space, and change over time, of integrated human-natural systems. As discussed in Objective 3.3, this activity is a priority of the NCA, and the Program as a whole can leverage the NCA's science-stakeholder engagement capacity to foster these planning efforts.

Box 16. Science for Water Resource Decision Making and Management

With the likelihood of drier, warmer seasons and increased droughts in many areas of the world as a result of climate change, water managers are faced with the challenge of continuing to supply fresh, clean water to growing populations. The ability to supply water is a particular concern in the U S. Southwest, where the population has nearly doubled over the past 30 years and where projections show an imminent transition to a drier future climate. Eight USGCRP member agencies are part of a Federal consortium that supports the National Integrated Drought Information System (NIDIS). NIDIS operates a Drought Early Warning System for the Upper Colorado River Basin and Four Corners Tribal Lands. Created via the NIDIS Act of 2006 in response to the need for long-term drought planning and a call from the Western Governors Association, NIDIS provides the best available information to enable users to determine risks associated with drought and provides supporting data and tools to inform drought mitigation. Programs such as NIDIS offer crucial input to decision makers who manage scarce natural resources, particularly in the face of large uncertainties about the pace and magnitude of future climate change.

USGCRP provides scientific underpinnings for NIDIS, including new observing and modeling capabilities and products. The Strategic Plan emphasizes the role of USGCRP in increasing understanding of the interactions between changes in climate and patterns in regional precipitation, runoff, and drought. In addition, USGCRP agencies will work to improve drought predictions over seasons, and even years ahead of time, by developing and using new modeling capabilities and better observations. These capabilities will improve information systems like NIDIS, which will in turn lead to better adaptation approaches for infrastructure planning, ensuring food and water supplies, and fostering stewardship of natural and managed ecosystems.

 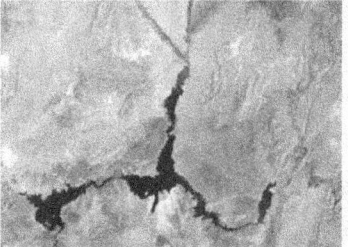

Figure: The eastern end of Lake Mead, August 1985 (left). In August 2010 (right), Lake Mead reached its lowest level since 1956, strained by persistent drought and increasing human demand. Lake Mead is the largest reservoir in the United States. Image courtesy of NASA.

Objective 1.3: Integrated Observations

Advance capabilities to observe the physical, chemical, biological, and human components of the Earth system over multiple space and time scales to gain fundamental scientific understanding and monitor important variations and trends

The research proposed for USGCRP in the next decade depends on the existence of a comprehensive, continuous, integrated, and sustained set of physical, chemical, biological, and societal observations of global change and its impacts. These observations are essential for improving the understanding of the components and processes of the Earth system and the causes and consequences of global change.

Observing global change in the Earth system is an inherently integrative activity. Effective observation of the Earth system and its changes requires remotely sensed and *in situ* observations from all domains—atmosphere, ocean, land, and ice-that are then transformed into products, information, and knowledge through analysis and integration in both time and space. For most measurements, no single approach can provide all the needed observations of sufficient quantity and quality, requiring coordination across platforms and instruments. In addition, such observations should be sustained in a well-calibrated state for decades (over multiple generations of observing systems) to separate long-term trends from short-term variability, and have global coverage at sufficient spatial resolution to account for variability across a wide range of scales.

The National Climate Program Act of 1978, the Clean Air Act Amendments of 1990, and the Global Change Research Act of 1990 collectively established systematic and process-oriented observations of Earth's atmosphere, land, ocean, freshwater, and ecosystems. The current observational portfolio upon which USGCRP relies includes satellite, airborne, ground-based, and ocean-based missions, platforms, and networks that provide measurements of the Earth system variables important for understanding global change. Revealing the characteristics and behaviors of Earth's component systems and establishing the existence of significant global changes are outstanding successes of the USGCRP agencies in partnership with the global science community (**Box 20**). The successes have been possible through collaboration and coordination among these agencies to harness their unique capabilities for *in situ* and remote sensing observation and monitoring and to sustain these efforts. The Program will continue to explore and develop opportunities for partnerships that maximize the effectiveness and value of observing systems to scientists, managers, and policy makers.

To achieve its goals in the next decade, the Program will build on these observational capabilities and achievements to:

- Sustain and strengthen the capacity to observe long-term changes in the global Earth system and integrate observations to improve fundamental understanding of the complex causes and consequences of global change

- Enhance the integration of new socioeconomic, health, and ecological observations with integrated observations of the climate system to address the vulnerability of ecosystems and human systems to global change and inform national adaptation and mitigation efforts

- Better integrate observations and modeling to advance both scientific understanding and decision support

In addition, USGCRP agencies have an important role to play in improving observational data access, sharing, harmonization, and credibility, as will be discussed in greater detail in Objective 1.5.

Sustaining and Integrating Earth System Observational Capacity

As discussed in Objective 1.1, the complexity of the global integrated Earth system is due to the interconnections between its components and processes, and to interactions across an extremely broad range of space and time scales. Understanding this complexity requires simultaneous recording of diverse observations, maintained over long time periods. USGCRP agencies and their international partners have made remarkable progress in this area. However, for this progress to be maintained into the next decade, the Program must work to sustain, and further strengthen, satellite and *in situ* observations to document long-term Earth system changes, for example in the Arctic (**Box 17**). Simultaneously, the Program must advance the integration of observational networks and systems to improve understanding of the linkages across components, processes, and scales that create the complex behaviors of global change.

Box 17. Impacts of Declining Arctic Sea Ice

Summer sea ice in the Arctic Ocean has been declining rapidly over the past several decades, with consequences for climate, coastal communities, and marine ecosystems. Ice loss means that highly reflective ice cover is replaced with open water, which absorbs more heat, contributing to the faster rise in temperatures in this region than anywhere else on the planet. This increased heating causes additional ice melt, accelerating the cycle of sea ice decline. Another consequence of reduced sea ice coverage is that an important barrier to storm surge has been removed, increasing coastal erosion and making coastal Arctic communities and marine life more vulnerable to the increases in stormy climate and coastal erosion. Later formation of sea ice in the fall and earlier melting in spring also limits the use of sea ice as a travel route or as a platform for subsistence hunting. Changes in sea ice extent disrupt marine food webs, affecting fisheries and threatening the economic base and viability of coastal communities.

Figure: Arctic char fishing. Image courtesy of Angsar Walk.

At the same time, ice retreat increases shipping opportunities and could open up more regions to oil and gas exploration. It also may contribute to increases in biological productivity in regions and in seasons not previously available.

To address the causes and consequences of reduced sea ice cover in the Arctic, USGCRP agencies will work together over the next decade to develop more accurate sea ice forecasts that permit local governments and managers to prepare, enhancing the long-term security of residents and local economies. USGCRP scientists also will work to identify best practices for building community and ecosystem resilience to the impacts of declining sea ice and help decision makers respond proactively to future changes.

Summer 1979 – Nimbus 7/SMMR

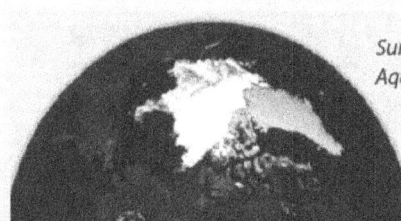

Summer 2010 – Aqua/AMSR-E

Figure: Summer sea ice extent in 1979 (left) and 2010 (right) as revealed by NASA satellites Nimbus 7 and Aqua using the Scanning Multichannel Microwave Radiometer (SMMR) and Advanced Microwave Scanning Radiometer for the Earth Observations System (AMSR-E), respectively. Image courtesy of NASA.

Continued investments in current networks are essential for this capacity and for achieving the necessary understanding of the Earth system and global change. These satellite and *in situ* networks, for example, measure the Earth's radiation budget, temperature, concentration of greenhouse gases, leaf area index, land cover, albedo, precipitation, winds, and sea level. Sustaining and prioritizing enhancements and extensions of these measurement systems from a climate and global change-related perspective over the long-term will be critical for improved understanding, tracking, assessment, and prediction. In prioritizing such investments, USGCRP agencies will focus on the linkage between research in key aspects of global change and those measurements most needed to improve understanding of the most pressing questions and issues, with a focus on minimizing the risk of serious gaps in global change monitoring.

A number of these observation systems are at risk of not being recapitalized or replaced. The risk of valuable information being lost forever increases every year that systems are delayed. Budget constraints and aging equipment, with their combined deleterious effect on data quality, reinforce the need for the agencies to continue working collaboratively through USGCRP in conjunction with the Administration and Congress to prioritize resources and then, by working within USGCRP, to leverage resources and set priorities, from critical satellite missions to the national stream gage network.

Furthermore, there are significant gaps between what is currently observed and the science priorities of the Program. Progress on global change science and response suffers from a lack of adequate time series observations of variables never before measured, particularly for key ecological and socioeconomic variables, as will be discussed in more detail. In addition, there are a number of existing measurements for which there are significant geographic or temporal gaps, such as ground-based snow cover measurements, especially in mountainous areas; terrestrial observations of ice caps, ice sheets, glaciers, and permafrost; and surface water and groundwater networks.

For many of these observations, integration of *in situ* and satellite measurements is crucial for calibration, validation, broader spatial coverage, and greater temporal resolution. One example for which these synergies are particularly important is greenhouse gases (**Box 38**). Although greenhouse gas concentrations are increasing in the atmosphere as a whole, scientists cannot yet reliably measure from space rapid fluctuations in their concentrations near the Earth's surface, leaving important gaps in the knowledge of the exchange of greenhouse gases among the atmosphere, the ocean, and terrestrial biosphere. USGCRP agencies will soon start implementing a plan to measure greenhouse gases throughout the global troposphere.

In implementing its observational strategy USGCRP will coordinate the many opportunities for leveraging existing platforms and resources to maintain the observational knowledge base and address key data gaps. For example, there are a number of measurements for which better calibration of operational sensors, or the mounting of new sensors on existing platforms, can reduce the reliance on separate research sensors. These are important ways of enhancing data accuracy in areas of high priority in the near-term.

Box 18. U.S. Group on Earth Observations

In 2005, USGEO was established under the White House Office of Science and Technology Policy's Committee on Environment and Natural Resources. USGEO coordinates Federal management of Earth observation and facilitates open and improved access for all of the programs of the U.S. government. It is chaired by representatives from the Smithsonian Institution and the National Oceanic and Atmospheric Administration.

Through USGEO, the United States further supports cooperative, international efforts to build the Global Earth Observation System of Systems (GEOSS). GEOSS is being developed through the intergovernmental Group on Earth Observations, a partnership of 80 countries, the European Commission, and nearly 60 international organizations. For additional information, visit http://usgeo.gov/

Another critical consideration for the next decade is that an increasing number of global change observations are now coming from instrumentation developed and operated by other countries. USGCRP will continue to expand its efforts to coordinate with international partners' programs so as to leverage investments, promote data sharing, and work toward a comprehensive international global change observing system. The Program must also continue to maintain effective partnerships with the other U.S. Federal interagency programs with responsibility for coordinating related aspects of science, technology, and the environment (**Box 18**). Similarly, USGCRP will coordinate with U.S. state government agencies that have complementary efforts such as state weather station and soil moisture networks participating in the NIDIS; engage nongovernmental organizations and the private sector in the design, deployment, and use of observations; and promote declassification of Earth observations for integration into the national civilian database.

Finally, the Program must confront the rapidly evolving nature of some global change observations, as a result of the explosion of the data collection capabilities of a large and growing array of "unconventional" platforms, such as smartphones, wired vehicles, and social networking sites on the web. These new sources of observations will offer significant new opportunities, not just for enhancing traditionally observed quantities like temperature and pressure, but also for data-driven ecological and social sciences information. Such new sources open up the possibility of detailed exploration of much finer spatial- and temporal-scale phenomena than otherwise feasible, including the initialization and evaluation of high-resolution models. However, transforming these data streams into information that is usable and useful for research is in itself a next-generation research challenge that USGCRP must confront.

Integrating Socioeconomic and Ecological Measurements

This Strategic Plan highlights the importance of ecological and social, behavioral, and economic sciences research for understanding global change causes, vulnerabilities, impacts, and responses. As with research on the physical climate system, this research depends on the availability of high-quality, long-term, and readily accessible observations of biological and human systems.

Box 19. A Socioeconomic Data Archive within USGCRP

The priority given by the USGCRP to integration of knowledge and models about both the natural and human components of the Earth system underscores the need for access to and integration of relevant natural and social science data in ways that facilitate research and inform decision making. A key USGCRP element is the NASA Socioeconomic Data and Applications Center (SEDAC), established more than a decade ago as part of the NASA Earth Observing System Data and Information System (EOSDIS). SEDAC is working to expand its data resources relevant to the USGCRP priority to improve understanding of the vulnerability, resilience, and adaptive capacity of human and natural systems affected by global change. SEDAC provides interdisciplinary data resources about key aspects of human systems and their interactions with the environment, including data on population, urbanization, agriculture, natural hazards, public health, income distribution, infrastructure, climate change effects, natural resource management, and environmental governance.

Data products and services are designed to complement remote sensing data (e.g., by identifying population distribution relative to measures of land cover, air quality, or ice extent). Other datasets available from SEDAC directly combine remote sensing and socioeconomic data, providing integrated measures of the interaction of human and natural systems that are aggregated to units of analysis useful for social scientists and decision makers, such as national-level indicators of population by climate zone or coastal proximity. SEDAC provides spatial datasets, maps, and online mapping tools to promote data access, visualization, and analysis. SEDAC also disseminates policy-relevant indicator datasets, including the Natural Resource Management Index, one of the indicators used by the Millennium Challenge Corporation in determining aid allocations.

SEDAC supports national and international global change assessments, including operation of the IPCC Data Distribution Center in collaboration with the British Atmospheric Data Centre and the World Data Center for Climate. Key data holdings include socioeconomic baseline and scenario data from IPCC special reports and assessments, and an observed climate effects database from the IPCC Fourth Assessment. SEDAC is also supporting the development of integrated indicators for the National Climate Assessment, and is promoting interoperable access to its data products and services through the Global Earth Observing System of Systems (GEOSS).

Observations of species ranges, migration, and interactions, biological productivity, ocean color, biomass, biodiversity, and ecosystem structure and function are necessary to assess ecological vulnerability and resilience to impacts. As with observations of the physical climate system, long time series with broad spatial coverage are required to measure changes and trends. The social sciences and ecological sciences communities are needed to help address many of the critical questions articulated in this Strategic Plan, but they are often hindered by the lack of available or easily accessible data.

A broad range of observational data about the human population, including economic productivity and consumption, health and disease patterns, insurance coverage, hazards exposure, and public perceptions and preferences, among many other topics, are relevant for developing an improved understanding of risk, vulnerability, resilience, and adaptive capacity. Some of this information is already available from the U.S. Census, for example, and from new social media and commercial systems, and could be incorporated in an integrated observations framework. Other data will require new observations systems and approaches that are critical for creating the integrated resources needed to meet scientific requirements. Such new observations would include detailed, place-based data about human behavior, attitudes, relationships, and institutions.

All of the aforementioned are important inputs to improved decision making about effective and sustainable responses to global change. Informing mitigation and adaptation decisions will demand the availability and synthesis of these data on an ongoing basis. Simultaneous, integrated observation of Earth system components will be necessary to track, understand and predict changes in agricultural productivity, energy production and use, water availability and quality, coastal hazards, biodiversity, and human health. It will also require these measurements to be matched to the scales of interest for researchers and decision makers, and made available in ways that facilitate whole-system analyses of societal and environmental interactions.

Achieving the integration vital to accomplish these USGCRP objectives will be challenging because of mismatches in the characteristic spatial and temporal scales of key processes and often widely differing characteristics of physical, biological, and sociological observational networks. Making such systems interoperable will be a major focus of the Program over the next decade, as discussed further in Objective 1.5. Such efforts will include creating common, geocoded geographic frameworks for observations collected according to, for example, both political jurisdictions and natural system boundaries. Furthermore, issues related to open availability and peer-review heritage for these disparate sets of observations, as well as the need to protect privacy and confidentiality for place-based social and economic data, make it more difficult to integrate them for specific applications. Meeting these challenges, however, will be essential for supporting assessment of vulnerability and informing decision making about responses.

In addition, as discussed, observation of ecological and social systems can be dramatically improved by collecting new kinds of data or using new data collection methods, including emerging opportunities to vastly scale-up the use of non-traditional data sources and "citizen science" research programs. For example, in the ecological sciences, citizen observer networks have revealed long-term, climate-driven trends in organismal phenologies (**Box 37**); however it will be challenging to integrate these measurement networks into broader observational systems.

Integrating Observations and Modeling

In addition to disciplinary and interdisciplinary research on fundamental Earth system processes; innovative computer programming; and high performance computers, networks, and storage, integrated suites of high-quality observations are needed to initialize and evaluate models. Many of the most important goals for the next decade, for example, significant advances in understanding the dynamics of how human causes of climate change interact with natural climate system variability, will likely result directly from the integration of modeling and observational activities of USGCRP agencies. The latest observations must continuously confront the integrated models of the Earth system to better understand the model limitations—the fundamental science they may miss, or misrepresent. New and improved observations of the Earth system for model evaluation will become especially critical as model resolution and complexity increase. Furthermore, new metrics that provide meaningful measures of confidence in models and their outputs for both scientific and decision support applications also will be necessary. Finally the research frontier of decadal climate predictability, as will be discussed, depends directly on assimilating observations, particularly of the ocean, into state-of-the-art climate system models.

The Program will also continue to place a high priority on limited-duration observational campaigns to aid in sensor calibration and improve process representation in the next generation of integrated Earth system models. In addition, it will seek to ensure sufficient observational focus to improve understanding and modeling of fast-changing environments, such as the Arctic, mountainous areas, and coasts, as well as provide focused observations for model-based assessments of short-duration, high-impact events.

Furthermore, integrated Earth system models help inform improvements in observations. Models help fill gaps in observations and identify optimum observational and monitoring strategies. All such efforts in model evaluation, the assimilation of observational data into models, and the application of models to inform observational improvements come with enormous data challenges that will be compounded by the increases in model complexities and the multiplication of the observational data required to test them. These enhancements will depend on advances in information and data management and sharing, as will also be discussed in Objective 1.5.

Box 20. Long-Term Observations Reveal Global Change

Analyses of sustained observations, often supported by USGCRP member agencies and their international counterparts, have been compared with pre-USGCRP observations, and demonstrate that the global integrated Earth system is undergoing significant and often challenging changes. Examples are shown in the diagrams to the right and discussed below:

- Annual mean atmospheric carbon dioxide concentration at the Mauna Loa Observatory in Hawaii is 20% higher in 2010 compared with 1960 levels. The rate of increase during the 2000s is twice as fast compared with the 1960s (p. 186).[1]

- The Antarctic ozone hole is starting to recover as atmospheric concentrations of CFC (chlorofluorocarbon) gases stabilized then decreased following the 1987 Montreal Protocol (p. 193).

- The 10-year average global surface air temperature increased by 0.8°C (1.4°F) over the past 100 years, with much larger rates of increase over the past 30 years (p. 206).

- Annual minimum sea ice coverage and annual average sea ice thickness in the Arctic Ocean have declined over the past 30 years (pp. 212-213).

- Global sea level is rising nearly twice as fast in 1992–2010 as compared with 1950–2000 (p. 238).

- Greenland Ice Sheet melting increased 30% over the past 30 years (p. 241).

- Over the last 50 years, precipitation has decreased significantly (15 to 40%) in the southeastern and southwestern United States, and increased in the northeast (10 to 20%), with an average national increase of 5% (p. 261).

- Northern Hemisphere snow cover has been decreasing over the past 80 years and the snowpack is melting earlier by as much as 20 days in the western United States (p. 261).

- The areal extent of global drought regions has doubled since the 1970s (p. 265).

- Large and long-duration forest fires have increased four-fold over the past 30 years in the U.S. western states and the length of the fire season has expanded by 2.5 months (p. 274).

- Locations of major fisheries in the Bering Sea have shifted northward over the past 35 years (p.282).

- The ocean is acidifying at an unprecedented rate (p. 285) with adverse effects on calcifying organisms, e.g., corals, clams, scallops, and oysters (p. 298).

- Stronger wind speeds and higher wave heights have been observed across the world's ocean over the past 20 years.[2]

- Nationwide, air quality improved significantly over the past 20 years for ground-level ozone, particulates, lead, carbon monoxide, nitrogen dioxide, and sulfur dioxide.[3]

- Tree growth rates are changing due to the rising levels of atmospheric carbon dioxide, higher temperatures and longer growing seasons (see also **Box 38**).[4]

---

1. Dr. Pieter Tans, NOAA/ESRL (www.esrl.noaa.gov/gmd/ccgg/trends/) and Dr. Ralph Keeling, Scripps Institution of Oceanography (scrippsco2.ucsd.edu/). Unless otherwise noted page references are to: National Research Council. 2010. America's Climate Choices: Advancing the Science of Climate Change. Washington, DC: The National Academies Press.
2. Young, I.R., S. Zieger, and A.V. Babanin. 2011. Global trends in wind speed and wave height. *Science* 332:451-455,doi:10.1126/science.1197219.
3. EPA. 2010. Our National Air: Status and Trends Through 2008. Available at http://www.epa.gov/airtrends/2010/(accessed September 16, 2011).
4. McMahon, S.M., G.G. Parker, and D.R. Miller. 2010. Evidence for a recent increase in forest growth. Proceedings of the National Academy of Sciences 107:3611-3615, doi:10.1073/pnas.0912376107.

Earth's Changing Environment

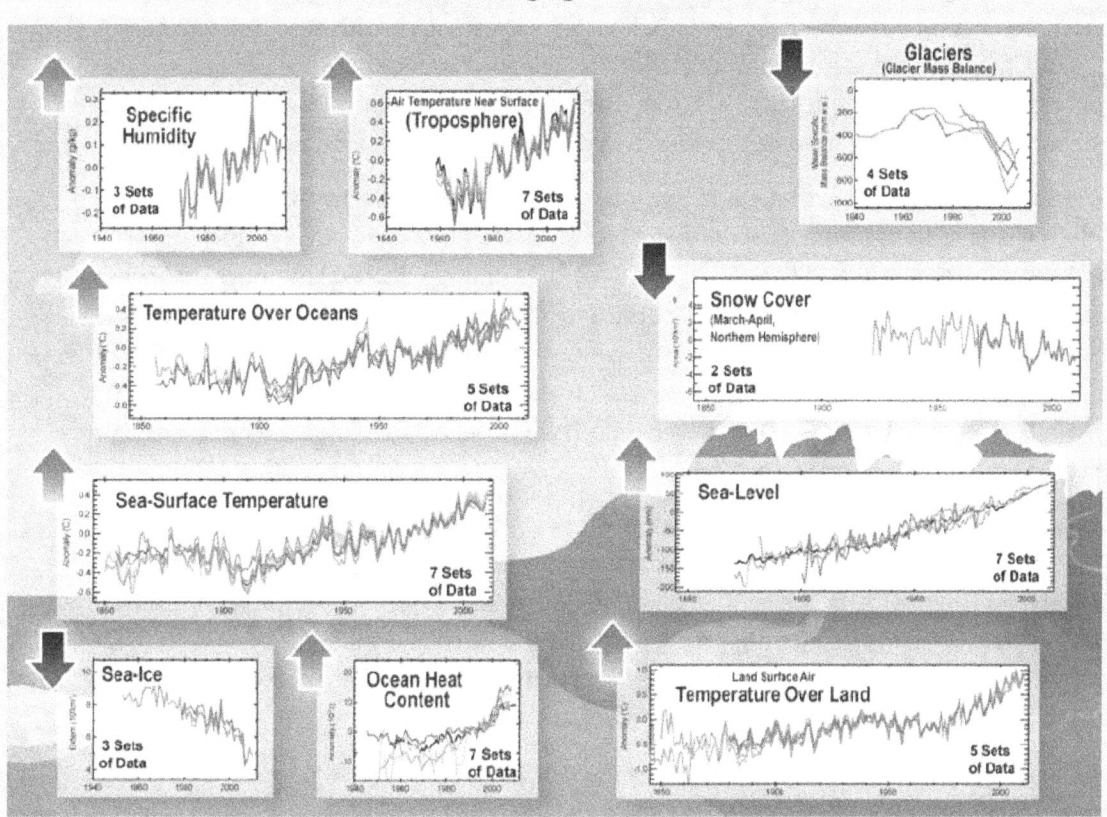

Figure: The ten most widely recognized climate indicators; vertical arrows indicate direction of change expected to accompany warming conditions. Each indicator includes all available peer reviewed products unaltered and unedited except for normalization to a common period of record to allow direct comparison. As illustrated, despite different choices in data sources and processing, all indicators point in the expected direction for a warming world. Time series plots are courtesy of John Kennedy, UK Met Office Hadley Centre, updated from State of the Climate 2009 (Arndt, D. S., Baringer, M. O. and Johnson, M. R., Eds., 2010: State of the Climate in 2009. Bull. Amer. Meteor. Soc., 91 (7), S1-S224.).

Objective 1.4: Integrated Modeling

Improve and develop advanced models that integrate across the physical, chemical, biological, and human components of the Earth system, including the feedbacks among them, to represent more comprehensively and predict more realistically global change processes

Modeling is an inherently integrative activity, synthesizing the understanding of the Earth system gained from theory, experimentation, and measurement. Efforts to develop models that integrate across Earth system components bring together researchers from many different disciplines. Efforts to use models to support decision making bring scientists and stakeholders into close collaboration.

Though the atmospheric, oceanic, terrestrial, and cryospheric components of the Earth system have been part of coupled climate models for a number of years, work is still to be done to advance the capability of such models to fully represent additional important features of the physical climate system. These include mean tropical sea surface temperature, patterns of variability in the large-scale circulation, the diurnal cycle of precipitation, and monsoonal circulations, among others. In addition, a number of Earth system components, such as ice sheets, aerosols, land hydrology, vegetation, and biogeochemical cycles, as well as socioeconomic drivers of global change, have to be included more comprehensively and dynamically in models to address critical science questions and decision support needs.

Advances in integrated Earth system modeling to address existing limitations, and achieve better integration, are both disciplinary and interdisciplinary, as they involve the representation of specific processes and the representation of the coupling among diverse processes (and methods). Improved process representation of Earth system components, as well as research at the interface between these components, will be critical for advancing integrated modeling. An important aspect of this will be improved coordination of observations, modeling, theory, and experiment.

To achieve all of its goals in the coming decade, the Program will address these issues by promoting greater scientific progress in the following areas:

- The development of complex, integrated modeling systems for improved understanding of the richness of Earth system interactions and feedbacks over a wide range of space and time scales

- The development of simplified and conceptual models for improved interpretation of these complex modeling systems in light of observations and theory

- The advancement of integrated modeling to support decision making through improved understanding of complex human-natural system dynamics

Model Complexity

The growing understanding of the complexity of the Earth system is in part reflected in the increasing complexity of the models. This increasing model complexity is often needed to describe Earth system processes and interactions more realistically. Earth system complexity creates a dynamic tension for modeling, between capturing as much of this complexity as possible for comprehensiveness and realism, and synthesizing and simplifying to grasp the fundamental aspects of a process, phenomenon, or system. In the next decade, USGCRP will play a major role in managing this tension and promoting balance between these two poles.

As described previously, the key to understanding the implications of and responses to global change is research that focuses on integration across Earth system components and processes and across space and time scales. Global change modeling reflects this integration, including the effects of human activities on the Earth system. The Program will need to foster the development of next-generation modeling systems that integrate more fully across all Earth system components and processes and allow for the development of more sophisticated and comprehensive understanding of the critical interactions and feedbacks of global change.

Enriching models to enhance their ability to capture both human and Earth system components is a major task that USGCRP will support through its coordinating role. Human system models relating to, for example, land-use change are undergoing constant development; additional efforts to develop energy and water sector models are highly relevant for developing global change scenarios. Given that improved information on population dynamics that affect water resources, for example, will be critical to support adaptation in the water sector, USGCRP will coordinate with the appropriate organizations involved in population dynamics and behavior. As models improve, additional characteristics, such as social networks for individuals, families, and businesses, will add complexity to models and improve their ability to represent a world that includes Earth system and human system attributes.

Continuing to place a high value on increasing model resolution in both space and time will be an important part of this effort. Increased resolution can have important benefits for both scientific understanding and decision support. Most generally, it will often lead directly to increased realism of a simulation (i.e., the extent to which a model can capture the full range of behaviors of the system). Increased resolution can also dramatically improve the integration of model components, as more of this integration can occur by explicitly and dynamically modeling key processes rather than relying on parameterizations that represent those processes in a simplified manner.

In addition, high-resolution modeling can help bridge the scale gaps inherent in global change, for example by nesting regional modeling systems within global ones. Such bridging of spatial scales can in turn create opportunities for eliminating some of the intellectual gaps between the science of the climate system and that of, for example, ecosystems, hydrologic systems, and human-environment interactions. This bridging of scale gaps can in turn foster bridging of the communication gaps that exist between global change science and the researchers and stakeholders dealing with issues of vulnerability, impacts, and adaptation at much finer scales. Similarly, incorporating additional process and impacts models into flexible Earth system modeling frameworks can enhance engagement, collaboration, and knowledge transfer across disciplines and the science-stakeholder divide.

Understanding interconnected phenomena with very different characteristic timescales, from diurnal and seasonal to multi-decadal and centennial, will also be a key focus for USGCRP modeling research. For example, the problem of understanding the potential impacts of long-term climate change on weather patterns and extreme events such as heat waves, precipitation extremes, and air pollution episodes will require improved fundamental understanding in a number of areas, including the links between synoptic-scale atmospheric dynamics and climate variability and change, improved representation of these links in models, and the archiving of model output at much higher temporal resolution.

One key issue when exploring the many possible dimensions of making Earth system models more complex and highly resolved is deciding how to prioritize such choices. For example, how does the scientific community decide whether to prioritize increasing resolution versus adding model components, in the context of factors such as simulation length, number of simulations, and amount of model output to archive, analyze, and visualize? These issues will continue to loom large despite the continuing expansion of computational capabilities. The global change research community as a whole would benefit from an increased and more systematic dialogue about this and related questions. USGCRP will play an important role in facilitating this dialogue around the guiding principle that decisions about investments in increased model complexity should be prioritized according to the value of information for both (1) addressing critical outstanding scientific questions, and (2) supporting decision making about global change responses.

Finally, whether it is improving the representation of currently modeled Earth system components, or incorporating additional physical, chemical, biological, or human components, processes, and interactions, achieving the next level of Earth system model integration will depend on advances in modeling infrastructure and frameworks. USGCRP will coordinate the development of flexible frameworks that promote modularity and interoperability in coupling together diverse component and process submodels. Such frameworks will be important for enabling parallel development of different model components, optimizing resources, and minimizing duplication of effort. In part, these activities will involve building on and continuing to foster efforts such as the Community Earth System Model and the Earth System Modeling Framework that rely heavily on grass-roots participation. Promoting the development and widespread use of such frameworks is a central task for USGCRP so as to maximize collaboration, co-development of models, and, ultimately, coordinate integrated research efforts.

Model Interpretation, Conceptual Modeling, and Hierarchies of Model Complexity

Just as large-scale processes have important effects at localized scales, small-scale processes in turn affect the larger-scale environment. It is important to emphasize that reaching down from coarse to fine resolution is not the only pathway for model improvement. Development of an improved understanding of how to scale up insights from fine-scale process and impacts models will also be important as will better understanding of the mechanisms that drive climate conditions, for example, ocean-atmosphere and land-surface interactions.

Modeling, in general, refers not only to the development of complex numerical codes, but also to the crafting of conceptual models that, through simplification of complexity down to core essentials, help bridge the gaps between observations and theory and between theory and scientific prediction. Highly simplified models can often aid in understanding and also help the more rapid development of sophisticated integrated modeling systems. In the next decade, the Program will work to promote the development of coordinated hierarchies of models, from simple to complex, to help the broader global change community derive the maximum scientific understanding and practical meaning from the large national investment in complex, computer-intensive, integrated modeling.

Given the great increases in model complexity and scope, it will become more and more difficult to quantify uncertainties in model results, for both scientific understanding and decision support. Uncertainty is an inherent feature of decision making, and its characterization can provide decision makers with a better understanding of available options. Meeting this challenge will call for greater USGCRP coordination among agencies and institutions nationally and internationally to address a number of issues. These issues include increasing the transparency of model assumptions and enhancing model reproducibility, assuring the continuing availability of enough computational resources to run the suite of models at the desired resolution and ensemble size, and covering the range of scenarios necessary to support policy making.

Integrated Modeling of Complex Systems Dynamics and Decision Support

Insights gained from applying the next generation of integrated Earth system models will support decision making for responding to change at global, national, regional, and local scales, for near- and long-term time horizons. To be most useful, however, model outputs will have to be aligned more closely with the needs of decision makers. The Program will facilitate this alignment, drawing from the large existing body of decision sciences research, and from Earth system science to improve understanding of key uncertainties. It will also help develop and apply new frameworks, to maximize the usefulness of its modeling efforts in decision support. Focus areas will include, for example, the derivation of regionally specific model outputs and production of model-generated information on short-timescale processes such as extreme events that have acute impacts on natural and human systems.

In addition, a fuller integration of certain human dimensions, in particular, the human drivers of atmospheric composition change, land-use change, and other dimensions of global change, into Earth system models is a top priority. This is also especially challenging. A key opportunity for USGCRP is to build on

---

Box 21. Integrated Assessment Modeling

Governments around the world, including the United States, would like to have as much knowledge and information as possible about how global change might affect their economies, jobs, public health, food and water availability, infrastructure, and natural resources. Integrated Assessment Models (IAMs) are tools that link natural Earth system processes and socioeconomic factors in a single modeling framework. They have proven extremely valuable in helping scientists and policy makers understand the interconnections between both the natural and human components of the Earth system.

One of the greatest strengths of IAMs is that they allow researchers and decision makers to explore a range of "what if" questions about global change impacts and responses. In the past, IAMs have been used mainly to analyze the effects of possible greenhouse gas control policies and technological advances in energy production. Today, however, these tools are being adapted to help policy makers make better decisions about natural resource management, infrastructure fragility, public health, land development, food production, and coastal protection that are all affected by global change.

USGCRP plays a leadership role in coordinating the development and application of IAMs to address this broad range of impacts, adaptations, and vulnerabilities, bringing together a wide range of the necessary social and natural science expertise from a diverse set of participating Federal agencies. Over the next decade, USGCRP will work with its agency partners to further develop IAMs and address current limitations. Such developments include, for example: allowing the models to operate at the appropriate space and time scales for new applications; improving methods for risk and uncertainty estimation within the models; developing interoperable modeling frameworks; and standardizing the input data sources for the many different IAM modules and components. These advances will have important benefits for both improving understanding of the interactions between human and natural processes and for informing responses to global change.

Integrated Assessment Models

Human Earth Systems

Economy	Security	Food	Forests
Population	Energy	Water	Transport
Settlements	Science	Technology	Health

Natural Earth Systems

| Atmospheric Chemistry | Sea Ice | Coastal Zones | Carbon Cycle |
| Nitrogen Cycle | Oceans | Hydrology | Ecosystems |

Figure: IAMs incorporate the connections between components of Human Earth Systems and Natural Earth Systems. Image courtesy of Jae Edmonds (Joint Global Change Research Institute/Pacific Northwest National Laboratories) and Robert Vallario (U.S. Department of Energy, Office of Science).

the insights and experience in this area gained from the development and application of Integrated Assessment Models (**Box 21**). The Program has the opportunity to ensure that fundamental advances in the modeling of Earth system components and impacts flow into advancing the sophistication and capabilities of these Integrated Assessment Models. This integration will have important benefits for both Earth system understanding and support for decision making about responding to global change.

Integrated Assessment Models to date have made emissions and land-use scenarios available for use in studies applying global climate models and have permitted analysis of the consequences of various proposed national and international emissions policies. However, Integrated Assessment Models can reach far beyond this application to provide a common framework for exploring the costs and benefits of adaptation and mitigation actions, the interactive consequences of these responses, and a combined risk perspective for decision making. The Program has an opportunity to foster the development of the next generation of Integrated Assessment Models that combine, within a common modeling framework, both the drivers and consequences of global change. USGCRP has a critical role to play in this effort, as it will call for significant cross-agency coordination to incorporate ongoing improvements in Earth system and impacts modeling into Integrated Assessment Model development.

In addition, there are many dimensions of impacts, adaptation, and vulnerability that are investigated within existing groups of research and practice, and with their own modeling tools. These include crop models, energy demand models, food-web models, water-quality models, human health models, models of human behavior, and models of the dynamics and genetic diversity of ecosystems. Such models should be integrated more seamlessly within global Earth system modeling systems, or at least made more interoperable with such systems.

Regardless of the type of model being applied in a decision support context, one particular challenge for many stakeholders and scientists is to articulate a role for modeling at the research-decision interface that goes beyond asking the question, "What is going to happen (in my country, state, city) in the future?" This question can be an extremely useful for decision making, but difficult to answer for aspects of the Earth system for which predictive capability is the most limited, such as biological and social systems, or for long time horizons for which uncertainties are large and potentially irreducible in the near-term. A key focus of USGCRP modeling efforts

Box 22. Decadal Climate Predictability

Planners at all levels of government and across all sectors tend to focus a great deal on looking ahead over time periods of a few months to many years. Examples include emergency preparedness, sustaining agricultural productivity, avoiding over-fishing, and maintaining infrastructure to ensure uninterrupted supplies of food, energy, and fresh water to communities and businesses. Planning outcomes in all of these areas and many more are very sensitive to season-to-season, year-to-year, and decade-to-decade shifts in weather and climate, resulting in the combined effects of natural variability and climate change trends.

Traditional weather forecasts only extend about two weeks into the future. Longer-term, less-focused predictions used in agricultural and emergency planning are only made about a year ahead of time. Because of recent advances in computing technology, combined with a new generation of Earth observations (especially of ocean temperature and saltiness), there is now new opportunity to explore the limits of climate predictability out to a decade and beyond.

Addressing the issue of decadal climate predictability will call for coordination across USGCRP agencies and the international scientific community. It will depend on effectively implementing and sustaining ocean, atmosphere, land, and ice observing systems; developing improved methods for using these data in global climate models; and applying advanced computing capabilities. It will also depend on enhanced cooperation between scientists and planners to ensure that development, testing, and communication of new scientific products and insights will ultimately be relevant for supporting better decisions.

over the next decade will be to better quantify these limits while expanding the range of benefits of modeling for decision support that do not explicitly depend on accurate, long-term forecasts of global change in specific regions and for specific socioeconomic sectors. Such benefits include:

- Hypothesis generation

- Development of bounding cases and "what if" scenarios

- Identification of potential warning signs

- Assessment of relative likelihoods and probable contingencies for future events

- Insights into trade-offs among alternative policies

- Identification of previously unanticipated vulnerabilities, including the potential for rapid or accelerating change and threshold-crossing in natural and human systems

- Improved understanding of unintended consequences

- Identification of robust policy options across a broad range of futures

The role of prediction will continue to be crucial in both research and decision making contexts. In particular, USGCRP will foster an understanding of regional climate predictability at seasonal, interannual and decadal timescales, focusing on spatial scales useful for regional and sector-based decision making, and at a temporal resolution appropriate for understanding changes in weather patterns and extremes.

As climate continues to change, predictive information on a variety of planning horizons will become important inputs into decision making for adaptation responses, in particular key planning horizons that are not so long that forecast accuracy is unverifiable, or that learning and feedback could not readily occur. In addition, it is widely expected that climate change over the next several decades will lead to a world with more frequent and intense extreme weather and climate events, such as heat waves, storms, floods and droughts. In such a world, managing competing demands on scarce resources and increased risks to vulnerable populations will demand improved analytic capacity across the board, including an improved capability for making relatively near-term climate predictions.

Finally, the Program will coordinate and enhance efforts to study climate system predictability over timescales of a decade or more (**Box 22**). Fundamental improvements in regional meteorological prediction on synoptic, seasonal, and interannual timescales, Earth system observational capabilities, and data assimilation approaches will provide the foundation for these new activities at the leading edge of global change science and modeling. Advances in decadal climate predictability have the potential to spur needed improvements in sector and regional impacts models, and lead to the development of new kinds of decision support tools for the new applications made possible by improved insights into climate variations and trends on these timescales.

Objective 1.5: Information Management and Sharing

Advance the capability to collect, store, access, visualize, and share data and information about the integrated Earth system, the vulnerabilities of integrated human-natural systems to global change, and the responses to these vulnerabilities

Over the next decade, achieving the Program's goals will depend on making significant advances in the Nation's global change information management and sharing capabilities. They will be vital for addressing the many dimensions of collaboration and coordination called for in this Strategic Plan. These improved capabilities, to capture, store, and integrate the rapidly growing data streams, as well as facilitate access and analysis of these data, have the potential to improve scientific understanding and aid in decisions that will lead to effective and sustainable responses to global change.

Although many aspects of data management have evolved over the past two decades, many challenges remain. Increasingly centralized data management storage and portal systems have been developed, but it is necessary to improve their organization, track data sources, and ensure data quality. There is also a need to improve interoperability among distributed data systems and to develop interfaces that permit integrated analysis. Furthermore, the ongoing explosion in data volume calls for development of user-friendly tools for access, analysis, and knowledge transfer. There is the potential for much more analysis, by many more researchers, of all of the data being collected and generated. There is a critical opportunity to learn much more about the Earth system by making it easier to analyze available and incoming datasets.

In the coming decade, USGCRP will provide a forum for its agencies to address all of these issues, sharing best practices as well as assuring interoperability and maintaining the flexibility to seize new opportunities for information management and sharing provided by emerging technologies. The Program must do more to transition to a new era of:

- Data-intensive science, where it is necessary to deal with both a huge amount and diverse sources of data about the fundamental processes and interactions in the Earth system

- Information-intensive decision support, where decisions about responding to global change harness the best and most useful information about the many interrelated factors that influence these decisions

Integrated and Centralized Data Access

With the advance of observational capabilities, computational power, and scientific research, there is both an opportunity for scientific progress in the study of the Earth system and a need to manage the data and information generated about it. USGCRP agencies generally have pursued a distributed data strategy over the last decade, in which individual agencies have established centralized archives for collecting and storing observational data resulting from their respective observational campaigns. This strategy of individual agency archive management will likely continue, as each agency, and its unique stakeholders, has specific data and information requirements. However, rapidly developing capabilities have created an opportunity to integrate across these networks to provide improved access and interoperability.

In the coming decade, USGCRP will take a leadership role in coordinating these networks, by providing shared data access, analytic capabilities, and modeling frameworks to support integrated research and decision support. For example, the Program is pursuing the development of a global change information system to support coordinated use and application of USGCRP knowledge and products (**Box 23**).

Specific issues that are imperative to be addressed to accomplish this in an effective way include data permanence, data volume and ease of access, data transparency and quality, protection of privacy and confidentiality for human systems data, data discovery, analysis tools, and community modeling.

Data volume continues to grow at an accelerating rate. Satellite instruments continue to collect a high volume of high-resolution (in time and space) measurements that are synthesized to create a record of the Earth system and its changes. *In situ* long-term network measurements provide valuable records of climate and environmental changes, often at high temporal resolution. Paleoclimate studies extend the historical record back in time, before that of instrumental records. Data from intensive field campaigns provide detailed information in particular regions. It is crucial to continue to collect and store these records, but this will also present data management challenges. As an example of the increase in the amount of observational data available, the NASA Earth Observing System Data and Information System (EOSDIS) archive alone has grown from approximately 100 terabytes (10^{12} bytes) in the year 2000 to approximately 4,600 terabytes in 2010, with comparable increases in other agencies' archives. Integration of new and emerging socioeconomic and ecological observations will add to this data volume, and introduce new challenges related to interoperability.

> ### Box 23. Global Change Information System
>
> The local- to global-scale impacts of climate variability and change, as well as the broader issue of global change, have fueled a growing public demand for timely and accessible information about present and future changes. Having scientific information about causes and effects of global changes helps people make informed decisions in their lives, businesses, and communities. USGCRP will lead an interagency initiative to build a new global change information system, providing timely and relevant data and information to stakeholders and the public. This system supports many objectives across the Federal government, including the National Climate Assessment. It will provide more timely access to information, the capacity to provide services to a much broader set of audiences, more transparency of data and results, and the ability to update information in real time.

As computational capabilities improve, increasingly sophisticated models provide the opportunity to evaluate regional global change impacts on multiple timescales. These models will continue to integrate more Earth system components, increase resolution, and be run in large ensembles. As a result, they are generating exponentially increasing output to be stored, shared, and analyzed. For example, during the time period that separates Intergovernmental Panel on Climate Change (IPCC) assessments, climate model resolution increases significantly, and the number of climate experiments conducted and diagnostics saved increases as well. The IPCC Fourth Assessment Report (2007) generated 35 terabytes of model data, but the upcoming Fifth Assessment Report is expected to generate over 3,000 terabytes of data. There is a similar explosion in reanalysis data sets, seasonal reforecasts, and seasonal-to-interannual climate simulation ensembles.

Addressing this data-volume challenge will require advanced technology to link users to the various data providers and cloud-based tools to facilitate collaboration. There are important existing efforts upon which the Program can build. For example, the Earth System Grid Federation is a data distribution portal that is currently used by many of the USGCRP agencies and international modeling centers. Its unified, virtual data-sharing environment links international climate research centers and provides a range of users with model-generated climate data, transforming distributed climate simulation data into a collaborative community resource. USGCRP will promote the access, search, and sharing of data by enhancing and expanding the use of such portals.

Human systems data will be crucial to the Program's integrated approach to global change research and described in this plan. Those data must be collected, well integrated into broader systems, and widely available. The social, behavioral, and economic sciences community has a long tradition of data sharing and research on which to build this effort, supported by a widely-accepted metadata standard (the Data Documentation Initiative), and led by sustainable data.

In this context, organization of data according to standardized ontologies, along with standards for cataloguing and inventorying metadata, will enable timely data discovery. The Program should continue to assist in addressing issues of data storage, transfer, and speed of access and analysis. Due to the impracticality of directly transferring and maintaining the metadata associated with these huge data sets, unified data portals will be most efficient if they allow users to work with the data close to its storage repository and extract and transfer only the needed results. Additional Program needs include continued adoption of standardized file storage formats for enhancing access to data elements, data transfer protocols that permit data subsetting and transfer, and service-oriented architecture at the data centers maintaining the portals. Analysis of large data sets depends upon the development of parallelized input/output methodologies, to facilitate rapid access to multiple stored data files.

All of the previously mentioned issues suggest prioritizing data and information transparency, provenance, and quality. USGCRP can play a leadership role in enhancing transparency and quality through efforts to ensure open access and provide authoritative products and portals. These endeavors will facilitate the efficient identification, access, and use of the highest quality data and information to support research about global change and decision making about responses. In addition, there is a growing collection of higher-level information about global change, and assessing its reliability is also critical. The Program must help ensure the availability of credible global change information, with attention to the depth of scientific detail appropriate for diverse audiences. In this context, USGCRP leadership in providing for an open data policy will be important, both nationally and internationally.

To help researchers keep pace with the growing data volume and the ongoing need to make information available to a variety of users, USGCRP will encourage the adoption of enhanced tools to categorize, synthesize, analyze, and visualize the data. Tool development must match the data level, application, and user sophistication. For example, the research community will increasingly depend on distributed analysis software (e.g., statistical tools) that can simultaneously access multiple observational and/or model data sets, taking into account varying spatial and temporal grids and data formats. Such software will increasingly require parallelization, as the data sets it accesses increase in size. Adoption of new, user-friendly, distributed visualization tools, including two- and three-dimensional maps, two-dimensional slice selection from three-dimensional fields, scatter plots for comparison of data sets, and feature tracking, will also be important.

Integrated Knowledge for Stakeholders and Decision Makers

Data and information about Earth system processes and societal vulnerabilities in the context of global change will be demanded by an expanding number of researchers, decision makers, and the public. Each of these groups presents a challenge to the Program to collect, store, publish, and serve this information in audience-appropriate forms. In general, these stakeholders often depend on information that is processed and synthesized.

In the next 10 years, the Program will address the unique information management and sharing challenges of providing integrated scientific knowledge in meaningful forms to global change stakeholders. Specific issues include integration of new types of data and information with Earth system data sets, and the development of new tools and methods for categorizing, synthesizing, analyzing, and visualizing integrated data sets.

As USGCRP agencies support efforts to respond to global change, they will generate new types of data and information that will be important to integrate with the Program's fundamental research findings and datasets. For example, the sustained assessment process (described under Goal 3) will encourage the development of integrated databases of stakeholder needs and the details of their adaptation and mitigation projects, efforts, experiences, and best practices for supporting decision making. These databases will assist in the development of readily accessible, comprehensible scientific information and promote enhanced communication, education, and engagement.

As is the case for the research community, the multiple global change stakeholder communities will also benefit from distributed analysis and visualization tools to synthesize and analyze diverse data and information streams themselves, as this will likely often be the most efficient pathway to the most usable information products. Currently, Earth system data use typically requires an expert understanding of the available formats, data characteristics, software packages, calculation methods, and visualization software. Non-expert users would benefit greatly from user-friendly software and simple modeling tools for a variety of informational and decision-support applications.

Finally, USGCRP will embrace the power of advances in information technology to transform public engagement with science and harness public participation in research, under the Communicate and Educate goal (Goal 4). Distributed computing, applications for mobile technology, and social networking have the potential to dramatically scale up citizen science where interested members of the public serve as observers, modelers, and analyzers of the Earth system, contributing to the scientific enterprise and broadening the meaning of global change in their own lives.

Box 24. Understanding The Role of Aerosols in Air Quality and Human Health

Aerosols are suspended solid and/or liquid particles in a gas, which can affect human health and the environment. Aerosol size ranges from several nanometers (nm = 10^{-9} m) to several tens of micrometers (μm = 10^{-6} m). Aerosols come from many sources, both natural and man-made (anthropogenic), including volcanic plumes, windblown dusts, sea-salt, pollens, and other biogenic particles. Anthropogenic aerosols include emissions from transportation, energy production, agriculture, biomass burning, and dust from road building. Aerosols are emitted directly and are also formed through gas-to-particle processes within the atmosphere. They mix with each other, undergo transformations, and are eventually removed from the atmosphere by various processes.

Quantifying aerosols and their effects is crucial for many reasons. Many aerosols are small enough to be ingestible into human lungs. Certain types may be more dangerous due to their chemical composition. Thus, aerosols and air quality are regulated and researched to protect human health. Aerosols are easily transported by wind and weather systems, adversely affecting air quality far from where they were produced.

From a climate perspective, aerosols are integral players. Again, due to their small size, they reflect and absorb solar radiation within the atmosphere, leading to reduced visibility. The same process that leads to hazy skies reflects solar radiation back to space, changing the energy balance of the atmosphere and hence climate. Aerosols can exert a net warming or cooling effect, depending on composition, placement within the atmosphere, surface type, and atmospheric conditions. For example, because of its dark color, black carbon (soot) released from burning of fossil fuels and biomass tends to absorb solar radiation and have a net warming effect within the atmosphere. On the other hand, sulfate aerosols are lighter in color and are more reflective, resulting in a net cooling effect. Globally, aerosols seem to provide a net direct radiative cooling, however the magnitude compared to global greenhouse gas forcing is uncertain and has a great deal of regional variability.

Aerosols are integrally involved within the hydrologic cycle (clouds, precipitation) because they serve as nuclei for cloud droplets and ice crystals and because they alter the thermal structure of the atmosphere. These perturbations change rainfall amounts and intensities. The specifics of the physical processes, and the actual magnitudes of these effects, including the regional and global radiative forcing of aerosol-cloud effects are among the most important uncertainties in climate science, and are significant areas of ongoing research.

Characterization of aerosols is difficult because of their relatively wide size range, diversity of composition, and highly variable sources. Unlike most greenhouse gases, which have long life-times and are relatively uniformly distributed globally, aerosols have shorter lifetimes and are concentrated close to their sources. This results in very heterogeneous distributions horizontally and vertically in the atmosphere.

Despite these challenges, there has been considerable progress made in understanding aerosols. Satellites are providing global and regional perspectives on column aerosol properties, augmented by aircraft and surface measurements to characterize processes and local properties. A major research challenge is combining continued global monitoring with new and increasingly sophisticated methods for measuring aerosol processes to understand the distribution, properties, and effects of aerosols across the globe, as well as how these will change with human activity.

Managing aerosols is critical for air quality and human health, as well as aerosol effects on climate change. Important synergies and trade-offs exist between air quality and climate, two different but interacting issues affected by aerosols. While it is easy to state that aerosols are "bad" for air quality (human health) and visibility, assessing aerosols for climate change is not as clear-cut. For example, since aerosols tend to provide a global reflective screen (cooling), they may be compensating in part for enhanced greenhouse gas (warming). Therefore, technologies and other measures intended to improve air quality by reducing surface aerosol emissions may actually unmask greenhouse gas warming. Identifying measures that both improve air quality and mitigate climate change is useful scientific input to decision making.

The Role of USGCRP

Evaluating such synergies and trade-offs requires significant amounts of information about fundamental aerosol processes and interactions in the Earth system. Over the past two decades, USGCRP efforts have led to considerable advances in this understanding, through enhanced observational capabilities, critical laboratory and

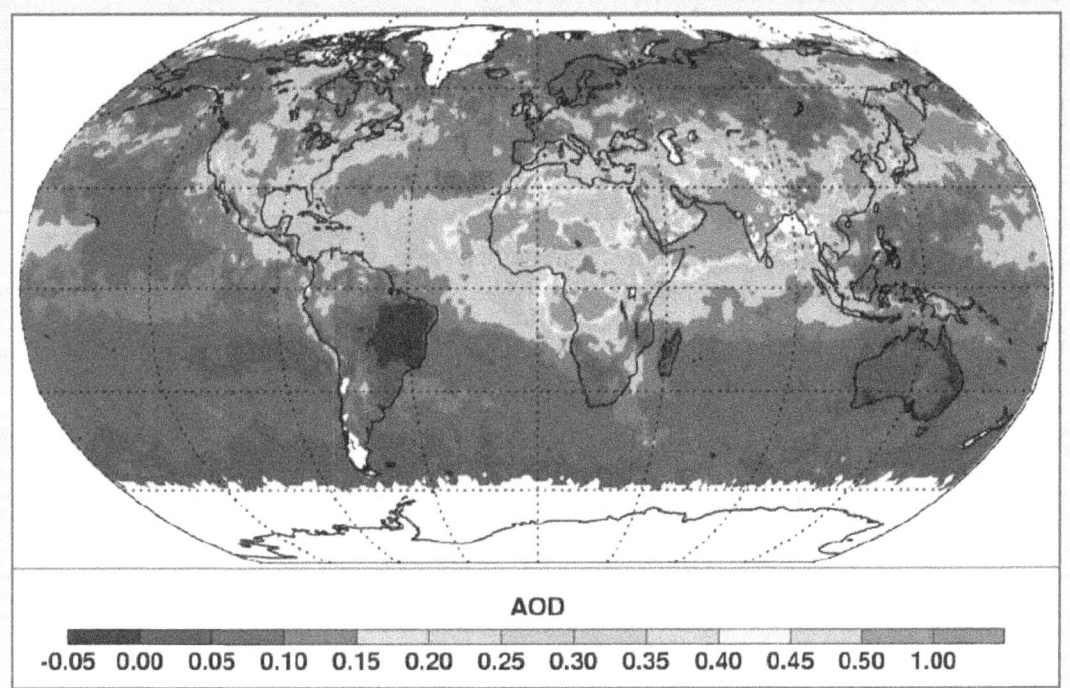

Figure: Global distribution of aerosol optical depth (AOD) as retrieved by NASA satellites during July 2008. The AOD is a measure of the interaction of sunlight and aerosols in the atmosphere, which is proportional to aerosol concentration. Higher concentrations are denoted by the warmer (redder) colors. Image courtesy of NASA and Remer, L.A., C. Brogniez, B. Cairns, N.C. Hsu, R.A. Kahn, P. Stammes, D. Tanré and O. Torres, (2012), Recent instruments and algorithms for passive shortwave remote sensing, in Aerosol Remote Sensing, Lenoble, J., Remer L.A. and Tanré D., eds. Praxis Publishing Ltd., London.

field experiments, and improved global model simulations. Much of this new knowledge has been disseminated through U.S. participation in international assessments (such as IPCC) and through comprehensive national reviews (e.g., SAP2.3: "Atmospheric Aerosol Properties and Climate Impacts"[1]).

In addition, operational partnerships through USGCRP have resulted in decision making tools that provide information to the public. One example of this is the AirNow website that provides operational air quality forecasts based on particulate matter and ozone forecasting across North America. NASA provides satellite data that feeds into air quality and meteorological modeling at EPA and NOAA to provide particulate matter and ozone forecasts important for sectors such as agriculture and public health.

Understanding the role of aerosols in global change remains a challenge. For example, while NASA's satellites have contributed to an improved picture of global AOD, they cannot conclusively indicate whether given aerosols have a cooling or warming effect on climate, or whether the aerosol comes from natural or anthropogenic sources. Continuing research and evaluation on questions such as the following are crucial for understanding aerosols and their impacts:

- What is the global distribution and composition of aerosols, and how do they vary?
- What is the role of aerosols with respect to cloud-aerosol interactions and the hydrological cycle?
- What are the net radiative effects of aerosols, and can they be categorized?
- What strategies can be used to limit some detrimental effects of aerosols (such as poor air quality) without adversely affecting climate change?

1. CCSP 2009: Atmospheric Aerosol Properties and Climate Impacts. A Report by the U.S. Climate Change Science Program and the Subcommittee on Global Change Research. Mian Chin, Ralph A. Kahn, and Stephen E. Schwartz (eds.). National Aeronautics and Space Administration, Washington, D.C.

Goal 2: Inform Decisions

Provide the scientific basis to inform and enable timely decisions on adaptation and mitigation

Global change is affecting many aspects of society, livelihoods, and the environment. Across the United States and around the world, people are making decisions to effectively minimize (mitigate) and prepare for (adapt) global change. USGCRP and its member agencies' past work on understanding the causes and consequences of global change has created a strong scientific foundation for informing decision makers who need science to understand and envision a range of potential impacts, risks, vulnerabilities, opportunities and trade-offs that are key for effective adaptation and mitigation actions. Over the next decade, USGCRP will incorporate a more decision maker-oriented element to the Program to better inform decisions—one that will conduct fundamental, use-inspired research; while delivering credible, relevant, timely, and accessible information.

USGCRP's success in informing decisions on global change depends on strengthening the dialogue and engagement between the science and decision making communities, with assessment being an essential tool (Goal 3). This collaboration and coordination at the interface between science and decision making requires new methods and a framework for multidirectional information exchange. Key elements of USGCRP's role in informing decisions are to:

- **Facilitate meaningful engagements between scientists and decision makers** with emphasis on assessing decision maker needs, capabilities, and science requirements; identifying critical gaps in knowledge and options for a use-inspired research agenda; and establishing new pathways for sustained dialogue

- **Provide access to relevant and accurate science** through an integrated set of user-friendly global change information and tools that leverage effective partnerships for multidirectional information sharing across and within scales (from local to international) and sectors

- **Guide and coordinate Federal science efforts through the USGCRP** to ensure they are useful and focused on relevant and beneficial societal outcomes

- **Inform Federal responses to global change** through close, ongoing interaction with Federal agencies and departments as they develop and implement climate change adaptation plans, as well as mitigation measures and policies, built upon sound scientific understanding

In developing a strategy for informing decisions, it is recognized that scientific knowledge is only one part of a much broader decision process. As stated earlier, information may be scientifically relevant without being decision relevant. In concert with the strategic elements described previously, USGCRP will help to define a framework for informing decisions that connects to the broader decision process. The desired framework will include approaches to assess the value of proposed decision support information, provide support for understanding risk management options, and communicate the variability associated with data and projections.

USGCRP will pursue its Inform Decisions goal through three objectives that build on use-inspired research advances. As such, they complement the Advance Science objectives that pursue fundamental global change research in support of decisions. Objectives 2.1 (Inform Adaptation Decisions) and 2.2 (Inform Mitigation Decisions) focus on new approaches for informing global change-related adaptation and mitigation decisions. Objective 2.3 (Enhance Global Change Information) focuses on facilitating these decisions by building an effective framework for global change information in support of decision making. For each of these objectives, USGCRP's strategy will leverage strong partnerships with the following: key local and regional entities, both governmental and non-governmental institutions, that have the lead in addressing climate change issues affecting vulnerable U.S. communities; resource managers across national, state, regional, and local levels who utilize comprehensive sector-based information; international organizations that bridge the gaps between scientific research, policy, and public action on trans-boundary issues such as water, pollution, and ecosystems, that impact U.S. interests (Chapter 4). Collectively, these strategic objectives will enable public and private leaders to routinely access and integrate USGCRP global change information, research findings, and assessments into their analyses and overall adaptation and mitigation decisions.

Box 25. Science to Inform Urban Adaptation

Strong partnerships and informed leadership are helping Chicago develop a response to projected higher future temperatures (especially severe heat waves, for example, potentially occurring as often as once every three years) that may affect businesses and the public. Using USGCRP agency data, a multi-stakeholder task force developed the Chicago Climate Action Plan, which identifies adaptive strategies to long-term climate change trends, such as helping property owners prepare greener landscapes and improve energy efficiency, and implements a more climate-conscious urban design to manage heat and flooding. For example, the City of Chicago is working to reduce urban heat buildup and the demand for air conditioning by installing roofs covered with soil and vegetation that are up to 77°F (43°C) cooler than nearby conventional roofs (Figures below).

In the future, USGCRP and its member agencies will continue to inform urban planning decisions by supporting the development of decision-relevant climate information. The Program will enhance the accessibility of this information through innovative knowledge-sharing tools like a global change information system (**Box 23**). USGCRP-supported assessments will provide researchers and community stakeholders with the opportunity to engage in a strategic dialogue to help identify knowledge gaps, project future global change conditions, and share information needs.

Figure: This infrared image, with a temperature scale on the right, reveals that "green" roofs are cooler (darker in color) than the surrounding conventional roofs. Image courtesy of Chicago Police Department and the Cook County Sheriff's Department.

Figure: The green roof on top of Chicago's City Hall is designed to cool the building and increase energy efficiency. Image courtesy of City of Chicago (http://www.chicagoclimateaction.org/pages/research___reports/8.php).

Objective 2.1: Inform Adaptation Decisions

Improve the deployment and accessibility of science to inform adaptation decisions

When considering options to reduce the risks of global change, decision makers need timely access to accurate and relevant information. Experience gained during adaptation efforts informs a research agenda that addresses the needs of stakeholders. In pursuing a more decision maker-oriented program, USGCRP recognizes the need for sustained dialogue that enables information exchange and feedback among scientists, decision makers, and practitioners throughout the processes of adaptation research, planning, implementation, and evaluation.

USGCRP will provide coordination functions to ensure that Federal science investments address adaptation needs. Emphasis will be placed on a continuous process for identifying information gaps articulated by decision makers, developing options for filling these gaps through a use-inspired Federal research agenda for global change adaptation, and exploring pathways for improved integration of science to inform adaptation actions. As a start, the NCA (Goal 3) is explicitly making an attempt to identify gaps in the research agenda.

USGCRP and its member agencies will also explore ideas and options for building capabilities in the deployment of accessible, actionable information and tools to inform adaptation decisions. As described under the Advance Science goal (Goal 1), these considerations will be particularly important in the development of methodologies and approaches to assess global change risks, impacts, and vulnerabilities, for use on local to regional scales where most management decisions are made. Such methodologies are also needed to assess the outcomes of alternative adaptation options and to improve approaches for identifying and managing for extremes, including low-probability, high-impact events. Exploring pathways for effective transfer of scientific knowledge to adaptation decision making will be guided in part by social science research that evaluates the uptake and ultimate effectiveness of USGCRP research into real world decisions. This research will occur at the interface between the science, policy, and management communities, supported by USGCRP coordination.

Key components for facilitating an effective engagement between the science community and adaptation decision makers include:

- **Assess and address decision maker needs and science requirements** by establishing sustained pathways and partnerships for continuous identification of the needs of adaptation practitioners, ensuring that these needs are addressed through a use-inspired Federal science agenda, and learning by experience what information is most beneficial to decision making

- **Identify and communicate relevant information** by developing and deploying a "map" of existing Federal science and services in support of adaptation

- **Develop new information exchange approaches** through efforts such as the creation of an online clearinghouse, or knowledge-management network, for global change adaptation and knowledge sharing

- **Support public and private sector responses to global change** through close, ongoing interactions as a means to provide readily accessible and timely data and information streams on global change risks and uncertainty. Particular focus will be on supporting Federal agencies and departments as they develop and implement climate change adaptation plans, as well as mitigation measures and policies, built upon sound scientific understanding

Governments at all levels play a crucial role in the development and implementation of global change adaptation measures and policies, and as such, provide immediate and long-term opportunities to institute and develop these components of engagement. USGCRP and its member agencies will work with state, local, and tribal governments, and other Federal agencies to build the capabilities for engagement and support needed by all decision makers, especially in key areas of vulnerability. One near-term opportunity for demonstrating these pathways is to provide information and assistance to Federal agencies as they work to develop and implement agency-wide climate change adaptation plans as mandated under Executive Order 13514: Federal Leadership in Environmental, Energy, and Economic Performance. By improving connections between science and decision making, USGCRP can play a valuable role in informing decisions.

Box 26. New Tools to Evaluate Sea-Level Rise and Coastal Flooding Impacts

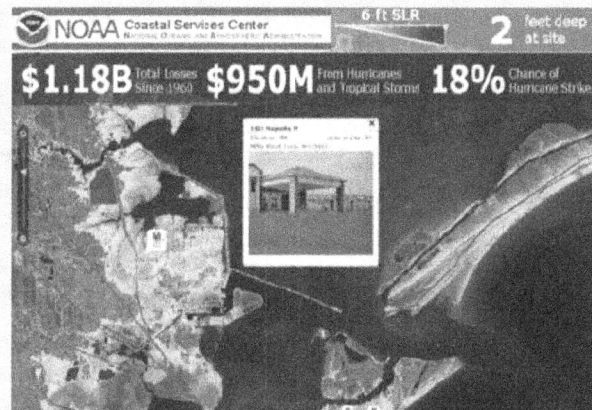

Figure: An image of a barrier island and coastline as seen via NOAA's Sea-Level Rise and Coastal Flooding Impacts Viewer at http://www.csc.noaa.gov/digitalcoast/tools/slrviewer/index.htm Image courtesy of NOAA.

Climate variability and change directly affect coastal communities. USGCRP member agencies are integrating multiple capabilities (observing, modeling, prediction, and decision support) and multiple scientific disciplines (climatology, meteorology, oceanography, economics, and social science) to provide these communities with a suite of global change information tools that will enable well informed decisions. One example of a climate information tool is the Sea-Level Rise and Coastal Flooding Impacts Viewer.

This tool provides simulations of sea-level rise at local landmarks, communicates the uncertainty of mapped sea levels, calculates potential marsh migration, overlays social and economic data, and examines whether tidal flooding will become more frequent. Communities can use this information for planning decisions in areas such as infrastructure maintenance, ecosystem management, and local business development. This tool and other information products will provide the real-time data needed to build resilient communities in the face of sea-level rise and other global changes.

Objective 2.2: Inform Mitigation Decisions

Improve the deployment and accessibility of science to inform decisions on mitigation and the mitigation-adaptation interface

Efforts to mitigate climate change have focused on reducing emissions of atmospheric carbon dioxide and other greenhouse gases. Approaches include more efficient use of energy, a transition to low-carbon energy sources (such as wind, solar, and nuclear), altered agricultural and forestry practices, and the capture and sequestration of greenhouse gas emissions. A recent study suggests that reductions in soot and methane may have short-term health, economic and climate benefits (see **Box 38**).[10]

To make informed decisions about mitigation options at multiple spatial scales, decision makers desire improved capacity to understand the effects of policy options on greenhouse gas emissions, the costs of reducing emissions, and the benefits of avoiding greenhouse gas emissions and associated changes in climate. Tools to inform mitigation decisions will be built on new research aimed at improving understanding of carbon storage in the Earth system, the development of scenarios of possible changes and impacts, and the identification of the social and ecological thresholds that help define limits to adaptation.

To be helpful to the broadest range of users, USGCRP science needs to be made available through tools, information, and practices that decision makers can understand and use. If mitigation actions involve market-based approaches, frameworks and inventories need to be in place to measure, monitor, and validate actual emissions reductions. Existing and improved inventories are important parts

Box 27. Construction and Climate

The construction industry needs information on climate variability and change in order to adequately anticipate the future likelihood of impacts such as sea-level rise or extreme weather events in the design of new construction projects. An example of how USGCRP member agencies have served the construction industry is in helping Boston evaluate the design and placement of their new sewage treatment plant.

Boston's Deer Island Sewage Treatment Plant was designed and built taking future sea-level rise into consideration. The level of the plant relative to the level of the ocean at the outfall is critical to the amount of rainwater and sewage that can be treated. To account for sea-level rise and to minimize later adaptation costs, the plant was built 1.9 feet (0.6 meters) higher than it would otherwise have been to accommodate the amount of sea-level rise projected to occur by 2050, the planned life of the facility.

The planners recognized the importance of using the best available information to plan future development. They factored the sea-level rise information to help make short- and long-term construction decisions that kept the project moving forward but would allow for improvements in later stages. For example, increasing the plant's height would be less costly to incorporate in the original design, or short-term construction phase, while protective barriers could be added at a later date, as needed, at a relatively small cost.

Figure: Deer Island Sewage Treatment Plant. Image courtesy of Massachusetts Water Resources Authority.

10. Shindell et al, 2012. Simultaneously Mitigating Near-Term Climate Change and Improving Human Health and Food Security, Science, Vol. 335 no. 6065 pp. 183-189.

of regular assessments that help inform national, state, and local policies (see also Goal 3, Conduct Sustained Assessments). The key components in facilitating an effective engagement between the science community and mitigation decision makers include:

- **Explore and address decision maker needs and science requirements** by serving as an interface between the science and decision making communities, including initiating new engagements for specific mitigation research issues and building the capacity for translating science for specific decision contexts, particularly risk management frameworks. Learn by experience with decision makers what information is most beneficial to decision making

- **Identify and communicate relevant scientific information** by analyzing and documenting current Federal capabilities for identifying, visualizing, and communicating existing environmental data to support management and mitigation science and service capabilities

- **Integrate Federal agency data and estimates of greenhouse gas emissions and sinks** at multiple scales for all sectors and regions and make available such information to decision makers in an appropriate manner. Pilot new information products and tools for mitigation decisions, including tools and metrics for evaluating the effectiveness of mitigation actions and tradeoffs (e.g., local land-use impacts to ecosystems vs. global impacts from greenhouse gas emission reduction)

- **Coordinate Federal agency research to inform the analysis of the impacts of greenhouse gas mitigation approaches,** provide transparent models and projections along with associated uncertainties to inform assessments of potential impacts of policies, laws, and societal challenges, over time utilizing results of research to measure, report, and verify greenhouse gas emissions

Mitigation and adaptation actions are inextricably linked via the future costs of impacts versus current investments in mitigation. The ability to manage greenhouse gas emissions through mitigation efforts will affect both the magnitude of the impacts to which adaptation is needed, and the effectiveness of various options. A better understanding of these linkages and interactions, through longer-term USGCRP efforts in Goal 1 (Advance Science), is necessary to develop effective adaptation and mitigation efforts and opportunities for co-benefits.

Objective 2.3: Enhance Global Change Information

Develop the tools and scientific basis to enable an integrated system of global change information, informed by sustained, relevant, and timely data to support decision making

A key task for USGCRP is to apply what has been learned from engagement with decision makers regarding the development and timely provision of information products, including forecasts, based on accurate observations and model results that help people make informed decisions. Optimally, these products should form an integrated set of global change information, derived from sustained, relevant, and timely data.

The local-to-global-scale impacts of climate variability and change have fueled a growing public demand for global change information. Such information helps people not only understand past, present, and likely future climate conditions (including natural variability), but also how those conditions affect their lives, businesses and communities. Easy, intuitive access to science-based information can assist people in making informed decisions to support economic growth, reduce risks to lives and property, and manage natural resources.

For the past two decades, USGCRP agencies have been providing global change information that is essential to many aspects of policy, planning, and decision making. The growing demands for information by decision makers, however, are highlighting the need for improved accessibility to more comprehensive, consolidated, and user-relevant global change-related data and information. Global change observations, monitoring, modeling, predictions, and projections—underpinned by the best-available natural and social science—can provide the framework of global change information. No single agency can provide the breadth of information needed. This provides a unique opportunity for current and potential USGCRP partners, including the private sector, academia, and other Federal agencies, to improve the effectiveness of its global change information in ways that better address the growing public demand for science that can inform decision making without prescribing outcomes.

To develop a set of accessible and useful global change information, USGCRP agencies will combine their scientific assets through scalable new partnerships for sharing knowledge, increasing public understanding, and building professional capacity. Recognizing the unique but complementary strengths of various Federal agencies, USGCRP is well positioned to connect climate science to decision making in a more disciplined and effective way. Agency efforts will provide data and information to governments at all levels, as well as businesses seeking to specialize in the provision of services and products based on environmental and climate data. USGCRP will prioritize such efforts by assessing the potential value to decision support as judged by the scientific maturity of the information and its relevance and timeliness with respect to specific decisions. It is expected that as USGCRP improves the accessibility of global change information, entrepreneurs in the private sector will be able to find new opportunities to tailor services to meet the needs of manufacturers, farmers, retailers, wholesalers, planners, resource managers, and others regarding how to adapt their business or community development plans to a changing climate.

USGCRP will seek to work collaboratively with partners, including decision makers in the public and private sectors, to provide relevant information for decision making from USGCRP's major goal areas in advancing science and sustaining assessments. The key components of the integrated set of USGCRP agency information products are:

- **Continually improve observing systems, data stewardship, and global change monitoring.** USGCRP agencies will collect, preserve, and analyze the global environmental record for continuous global change monitoring and develop periodic assessments in support of informed decisions. This readily accessible, long-term archive will serve the Nation's need for trusted global change-related information about the past, current and changing state of the Earth system and provide the basic foundation for decision makers. A global change information system will be an important step in this direction (**Box 23**).

- **Translate global change predictions and projections.** USGCRP global change predictions and projections will provide information on impacts from shorter-term climate variability and longer-term changes. Experimental analysis and translation tools will be developed with stakeholders to transform model projections into useful information at relevant spatial and temporal scales.

- **Provide timely, relevant, and integrated global change information and decision support.** USGCRP and its member agencies will provide timely and relevant global change information to other Federal programs that address global change-related issues on various scales, from local, regional, and national to international. In addition, USGCRP will deliver data and information streams (designed to support specific decisions in regions and sectors) to the public and to climate service providers that develop decision-support tools and other applications.

USGCRP will strive to ensure that the best-available global change information and tools will be delivered to support public and private sector policy, planning, and decision making. Scenario-based modeling approaches will continue to be an important direction for global change research. Effective application of scenarios in decision support will require strong stakeholder engagement to help facilitate careful explanation of the assumptions that underlie the scenarios and the communication of quantitative estimates of uncertainties in simulation outputs. This will be most relevant for improving decision outcomes, as high-resolution integrated Earth system models are extraordinarily complex.

Because many global change information products are being provided today by national, state, and municipal agencies, as well as by agencies outside the government, a key challenge for USGCRP will be to develop more effective coordination, communication and resultant synergy among these bodies. As an example, USGCRP will work closely with the Global Framework for Climate Services (GFCS) in defining a set of international arrangements that would lead to better climate-related information products for decision making in an international context. The Nation's need for global change information exceeds the scope of any individual organization or agency. Accordingly, a strong USGCRP-led framework for inter-agency and external partnerships is critical to satisfying the need for relevant global change information.

USGCRP can profoundly advance the Nation's capacity to apply scientific information to the strategic choices faced by decision makers in the context of global change. The best science will only benefit society when there is an ongoing process that evaluates the accessibility and use of the science for decision makers. USGCRP will strengthen connections between global change science, assessments, and decision making by ensuring a responsive science agenda that meets decision maker needs, developing information pathways that support institutional decisions, engaging in ongoing evaluations of program effectiveness, and leveraging domestic and international capabilities and partnerships.

USGCRP's activities to inform decisions in a changing global environment will be conducted in coordination with its other goals: advancing science, conducting sustained assessments, and enhancing communication and education. Together, these strategic efforts will ensure that scientific information is timely, credible, relevant, and accessible, and that science is continuously and effectively communicated to planners and decision makers across all levels and sectors.

Box 28. Growing Seasons

The agriculture industry in the United States generates over $200 billion a year in food and commodities from a diverse range of crops and animals. Climate change affects this industry by contributing to increased productivity in certain crops and reducing productivity in others.

Crop responses in a changing climate reflect the interplay among three factors: changing temperatures, changing water resources, and increasing carbon dioxide concentrations as they affect the crops and also crop pests. Warming generally causes plants that are below their optimum temperature to grow faster, with obvious benefits. For some plants, such as cereal crops, however, faster growth means there is less time for the grain itself to grow and mature, reducing yields. For some annual crops, adjusting the planting date to avoid late season heat stress is one strategy for adjusting to changes.

The grain-filling period (the time when the seed grows and matures) of wheat and other small grains shortens dramatically with increasing temperatures. Analysis of crop responses suggests that even moderate increases in temperature will decrease yields of corn, wheat, sorghum, bean, rice, cotton, and peanut crops.

Changing numbers of freezing days provide another example of how agriculture is affected by climate change. Since the mid-1970s, observations show that the number of days per year in which the temperature falls below freezing has declined by four to seven days over much of the Southeast. Some areas, such as western Louisiana, have experienced more than 20 fewer freezing days. These observations can help inform farmers and others in the agriculture business to maximize their crop output. For scientists, these observations inspire future research around climate to continue to inform decision makers: Will these trends continue, accelerate, or change direction? How will next year's freeze-free period compare to these trends?

USGCRP will coordinate efforts of member agencies that, through observations, crop- and forest-growth models, and regional climate models, will provide authoritative information and tools that can be used by farmers and landowners to make decisions relevant to agricultural production in a changing climate.

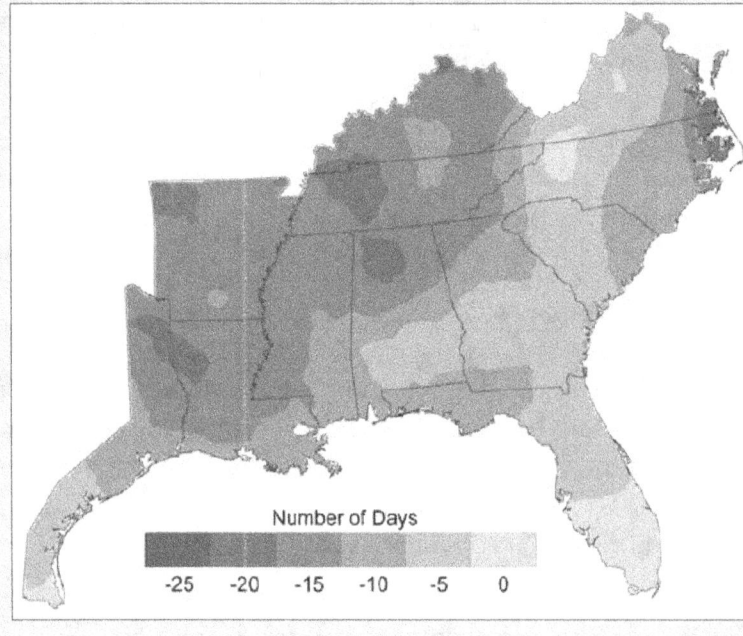

Number of Days

-25   -20   -15   -10   -5   0

Figure: Since the mid-1970s, the number of days per year in which the temperature falls below freezing has declined by four to seven days over much of the Southeast. Some areas, such as western Louisiana, have experienced more than 20 fewer freezing days. Climate models project continued warming across the region, with the greatest increases in temperature expected in summer, and the number of very hot days increasing at a greater rate than the average temperature. Image courtesy of NOAA/NCDC.

Goal 3: Conduct Sustained Assessments

Build sustained assessment capacity that improves the Nation's ability to understand, anticipate, and respond to global change impacts and vulnerabilities

Assessments are essential tools for linking science and decision making. They survey, integrate, and synthesize science, within and between scientific disciplines and across sectors and regions. Assessments support the critical analysis of issues, highlighting key knowledge that can improve policy choices and identifying significant gaps that can limit effective decision making. They are vehicles for sustained dialogue among stakeholders, who are typically decision makers, scientists or other experts across the country. Assessment activities also track progress by identifying changes in the condition of the integrated Earth system over time, advances in the underlying science, and changes in human response. As a result, they are critical elements in achieving USGCRP's vision.

Assessments have been integral components of USGCRP since its inception. Individual agencies also regularly use assessments to ensure that the agencies are meeting their legal mandates, and to deploy the best available science toward achieving their missions. Additionally, along with its strategic role as coordinator of Federal global change research, USGCRP is required by the Global Change Research Act of 1990 to conduct a National Climate Assessment (NCA, **Box 29**). USGCRP also coordinates and supports U.S. participation in appropriate international assessment efforts, such as the IPCC. USGCRP has the capacity, resources, and interest for comprehensive national and international assessment of global change, and provides a link to U.S. participation in other assessments.

> ### Box 29. National Climate Assessment
>
> The USGCRP is required on a periodic basis (not less frequently than every 4 years) to submit to the President and the Congress a report that:
>
> - Integrates, evaluates, and interprets the findings of the USGCRP and discusses the scientific uncertainties associated with such findings;
>
> - Analyzes the effects of global change on the natural environment, agriculture, energy production and use, land and water resources, transportation, human health and welfare, human social systems, and biological diversity; and
>
> - Analyzes current trends in global change, both human-induced and natural, and projects major trends for the subsequent 25 to 100 years.
>
> - Global Change Research Act of 1990

The National Context

USGCRP agencies have long employed assessments as tools to support decision making based upon scientific outcomes. Keys to success include careful stakeholder interaction, development of indicators on status and trends of key variables and values, and adaptive management of the assessment process. Climate change adds an additional stress to environments already experiencing multiple global change and other stresses (e.g., population growth, land use change, urbanization, and industrialization). Encompassing climate in assessments is further complicated by the need to account for regional differences in climate change impacts. Many entities are conducting risk-based assessments of their vulnerability to existing stresses, including extreme events, and are beginning to evaluate how climate alters the risks (e.g., 100-year floods). Within the Federal government, strategies for adaptation and mitigation will be supported by explicitly focusing on the science and decision support needs of the Federal agencies as information is developed for the NCA. Not only is the Federal government a key partner in the Nation's efforts to adapt to climate change, it also has a direct stake in adaptation because climate change directly affects Federal services, operations, and programs across the country.

To improve effectiveness and regional coordination, the Council on Environmental Quality (CEQ), the Office of Science and Technology Policy (OSTP), and USGCRP are working together to leverage capacity

and expertise of existing institutions, while providing flexibility to reflect the regional context, including differences in issues, assets, and capabilities. Strong Federal research programs in eight identified regions (or "hubs") will engage with existing Federal and non-Federal partners throughout each region to coordinate global change science and information, connect decision makers and climate experts, and engage a broad range of stakeholders (**Box 30**). This hub network approach should greatly facilitate the employment of common standards and information across the Nation. Employing common standards will, in turn, enhance understanding of projections of climate impacts and promote best practices to adapt to future climate.

USGCRP is responsible for satisfying the legal mandate of the Global Change Research Act for an NCA. The NCA is the USGCRP process that will produce an ongoing, comprehensive assessment of climate and global change for the Nation, including impacts, vulnerabilities, and response strategies, within a context of sustainable and environmentally sound development paths for communities and the Nation as a whole.

In addition to the requirements of the Global Change Research Act to address specific components of natural and societal systems, assessments must account for the effects of global change where it directly impacts the lives of citizens, in their geographic regions, and so the NCA includes analyses within regions of the country as an integral component. The NCA is also nested within a global context and connected to the international assessments whose activities are supported by USGCRP. The NCA develops focused investigations of regional and sectoral topics, as well as integrated topics that have high priority due to existing or anticipated climate

> ### Box 30. The Federal Role in Making Regional Knowledge Accessible
>
> The USGCRP Strategic Plan calls for enhanced coordination and cooperation among the Federal global change science and service programs to realize its vision and contribute to a government-wide approach to global change. This vision is responsive to a shared and clearly expressed need from communities across the United States for climate information and services to enable better planning and management of the risks of global change to people, places, and the economy. As a part of this vision, USGCRP and its member agencies will meet regional needs arising from local communities' specific socio-economic, environmental, and cultural contexts.
>
> Planning is already underway, guided by the CEQ and the OSTP, to better use the capacity of existing institutions of the Federal government and key partners to more efficiently and effectively deliver regional knowledge. The USGCRP Strategic Plan goals Inform Decisions and Conduct Sustained Assessments are carefully designed with this regional coordination effort in mind. For instance, eight identified regions for the NCA are identical to those used in the CEQ and OSTP adaptation efforts. This shared approach will result in USGCRP's improved ability to offer access to Federal climate information, tools, and resources specific to each region and across regions, and to engage information users in a collaborative and inclusive process of using and creating knowledge. USGCRP will support the development of regional adaptation strategies by strengthening the connections between Federal science and information users, and strengthening the pathways by which stakeholder needs are incorporated into research priorities.

stresses. These nested investigations allow for a more detailed and focused assessment of issues in specific locations and within natural and human systems. Finally, because of the complexity of climate change, national and international assessments are expected to prioritize issues that cut across traditional topics and institutional boundaries. Tackling issues that cut across institutional boundaries requires consideration of geographically and biophysically defined regions such as arid lands and coasts, and interactions between the natural and built environments (e.g., the nexus of energy, water, and land), as well as recognition that the United States is embedded within an increasingly complex matrix of international relationships.

The strategic vision for the NCA differs in multiple ways from previous U.S. climate assessment efforts.[11] Building on the recommendations of the National Research Council, it will implement a long-term, consistent, and ongoing process for evaluation of climate risks and opportunities, and informing decision making processes within regions and sectors. An essential component of this process is to establish sustained assessment activity both inside and outside of the Federal government that draws upon, and sustains, the work of stakeholders and scientists across the country. A sustained assessment process is most appropriate to effectively respond to the four-year reporting requirement of the Global Change Research Act, and will reduce the need for the lengthy reports of past assessments. It will also be more focused on evaluating the current state of scientific knowledge relative to climate impacts and trends, and on supporting the Nation's activities in adaptation and mitigation.

The NCA will no longer envision climate change as an independent risk, but as an additional factor to existing risk-based assessments, while recognizing new impacts such as ocean acidification. It will lead the development of a small, consistent suite of indicators of climate change that encompass metrics for progress in adaptation and mitigation activities using a risk-based framing. The NCA will also be the initial focal point for development of the USGCRP interagency global change information system that will provide timely, authoritative, and relevant information, and produce reports and web-based products that are useful for decision making at multiple levels (**Box 23**).

The benefits of these new approaches to assessment include increased efficiency and leveraging of existing resources within USGCRP, deeper stakeholder involvement, broader distribution of new ideas and best practices, a process to feed back information from users into the science priorities, and improved capacity to cope with global change. The resulting infrastructure, protocols, and tools will be available more widely to enable assessment processes across multiple scales and sectors, conducted outside the USGCRP.

The International Context

USGCRP recognizes the international context of climate trends and the connections between risks and vulnerabilities to the United States that are generated by climate impacts elsewhere. Obviously, adaptation and mitigation decisions within the United States have impacts on other countries, and vice versa. These impacts occur within ecological, physical, social, and political systems that affect countries across the globe, and so the United States should remain fully engaged with the international community given the strategic importance of global trade, security, and diplomacy.

USGCRP and its member agencies will continue to play a pivotal role in coordinating and supporting the active engagement of the Nation's scientific community in appropriate international assessments, to ensure, among other things, that U.S. national interests are represented. The Program coordinates and supports U.S. scientists' participation in, and government and expert review of, the global assessment

11. For more information, visit http://globalchange.gov/what-we-do/assessment/nca-reports

of the climate through the IPCC, providing strong intellectual input to the process. The NCA activities will be coordinated with the efforts of the IPCC to maximize the benefit of work products from each to the other. Similarly, USGCRP will also continue to act as a nexus for agency participation in other international assessments of global change, such as the Arctic Climate Impact Assessment and the Scientific Assessment of Ozone Depletion (**Box 33**).

In addition to global-scale assessments, USGCRP will work with neighboring nations to enhance joint successes. For instance, the U.S. regional hubs will need to engage with their international neighbors on issues ranging from water resources, to biological invasions and habitat shifts, to energy and transportation. Promoting scientific diplomacy can be a catalyst for other U.S. initiatives while also streamlining implementation of adaptation and mitigation activities. Extending beyond the Nation's immediate boundaries, USGCRP assessments should also account for climate impacts on markets and people worldwide due to the increasingly complex fabric of international commerce.

Connections to Other Goals

Assessments support achievement of all of the other goals of the USGCRP Strategic Plan. For instance, they organize thinking, identify gaps in scientific understanding and highlight new scientific findings (Goal 1: Advance Science). Another important overlap with Advance Science is the critical issue of data management and deployment, as well as promoting interoperability and integration of climate-related information that is generated from a variety of sources (**Box 23**). Similarly, the NCA will help synthesize and integrate scientific information for decision making related to global change across all sectors, regions, and scales, and improve the deployment and accessibility of science-based information to inform adaptation and mitigation decisions (Goal 2: Inform Decisions). Successful assessment should establish sustained engagement among multiple stakeholders to enable effective decision making, which clearly overlaps with the central features of Goal 4 (Communicate and Educate) to reach diverse audiences and to establish effective engagement. Additionally, the NCA process will advance a scientific workforce capable of addressing multi-stressor, cross-sectoral issues and the appropriate transfer of that scientific knowledge to communities engaged in adaptive risk management.

In addition to coordination with the other USGCRP Strategic Plan goals, achieving this goal requires successful responses to four objectives whose interacting elements support a comprehensive national assessment process, respond to the Global Change Research Act, and provide a platform for U.S. participation in international assessments. These elements include:

- Full integration of the best scientific knowledge

- Development and deployment of an ongoing assessment process

- Ensuring the capture of relevant information to inform decision making

- Continuous evaluation of progress and employing adaptive management over time

Box 31. Vulnerability Assessment and Climate Change Adaptation in New York City

Projections for New York City (NYC) suggest that by mid-century, up to two feet (0.6 meters) of sea-level rise will increase the frequency of flooding and impacts of storm surge in many areas of the city – if adaptation measures are not taken. In preparation for such a scenario, NYC undertook a city-wide risk assessment using historical tide gauge data, climate model outputs, recent ice melt, and paleoclimate data. NYC decision makers were engaged throughout the risk assessment to ensure that climate information was linked to adaptation planning. This involvement is helping to foster new approaches that include urban planning and architectural perspectives.[12] It serves as a model for the science-stakeholder interaction that will increasingly inform USGCRP science, and for the development of user-friendly climate information.

Sea-level and climate modeling supported by USGCRP agencies and included in IPCC projections are critical for risk assessment efforts such as the one New York City undertook. USGCRP will develop global change models that provide information at the regional scale— the scale at which many adaptation decisions are made. USGCRP will also develop information services to ensure that scientific advances are useful and accessible to decision makers and managers.

Figure: The light blue area depicts today's FEMA 100-year flood zone for the city (the area of the city that is expected to be flooded every 100 years). With rising sea levels, more frequent flood events will inundate this area and a 100-year flood is projected to inundate a far larger area of New York City, especially under the higher emissions scenario. Critical transportation infrastructure located in the Battery area of lower Manhattan could be flooded far more frequently unless protected. The increased likelihood of flooding is causing planners to look into building storm-surge barriers in New York harbor to protect downtown New York City. Image courtesy of New York City, Applied Science Associates, Inc.

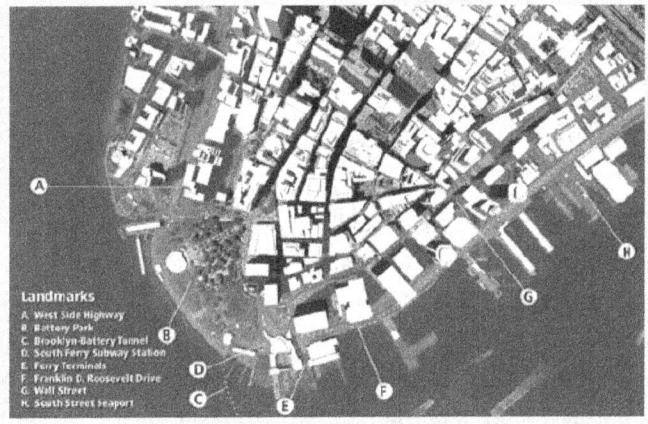

Landmarks
A. West Side Highway
B. Battery Park
C. Brooklyn-Battery Tunnel
D. South Ferry Subway Station
E. Ferry Terminals
F. Franklin D. Roosevelt Drive
G. Wall Street
H. South Street Seaport

Objective 3.1: Scientific Integration

Integrate emerging scientific understanding of the integrated Earth system into assessments and identify critical gaps and limitations in scientific understanding

Through the scientific endeavor, USGCRP will continue to develop capacity to understand observed climate events and trends, as well as to realistically project forward into the future (Goal 1). Assessments provide the opportunity for regular analysis and synthesis of the wealth of scientific data and understanding collected across the breadth of USGCRP agencies, all levels of government, the academic community, and the nonprofit and business sectors. Integrating and synthesizing the knowledge base on a regular basis is crucial for informed adaptation, mitigation, and planning decisions, both nationally and internationally.

Integrating climate science into assessments also helps identify critical gaps in knowledge. For instance, Impacts, Adaptation, Vulnerability (IAV) models help formulate the understanding of the impacts of change and the scope for adaptation of vulnerable populations or ecosystems (see Objective 1.4: Integrated Modeling), but they need improvement to cope with the longer timescale of climate change.

12. Rosenzweig, C., and Solecki, W. eds., 2010. Climate Change Adaptation in New York City: Building a Risk Management Response. New York City Panel on Climate Change 2010 Report. *Annals of the New York Academy of Sciences*, v. 1196.

This integration of science and assessments is then used to assess options and prioritize investments in science and other Federal activities to maintain a sustained and coordinated research program that is responsive to both the Global Change Research Act and other ongoing assessment needs. The identification of science needs should include physical, ecological, health, and social science components that will allow prioritization of investments in adaptation and mitigation activities over the next decades. There is a particular need to continue to build the social science base for analysis of risks, vulnerabilities and adaptation options, as developed under Advance Science and Inform Decisions goals.

As the Nation moves forward to adapt to global change, the NCA needs to synthesize knowledge associated with adaptation and mitigation, and identify best practices from around the country and the globe, including risk-based approaches to community resilience and disaster preparedness. For example, local entities have long considered a suite of weather risks and codified engineering standards for them, but those baselines are now shifting. The NCA will identify and highlight how communities of practice are realigning to the latest scientific knowledge. Components of the assessment reports should also integrate information to facilitate making the best decisions under uncertainty given the long timeline of global change and its impacts.

The full panoply of scientific understanding, including social, behavioral, economic, ecological, and physical, will be applied to regional, sectoral, and crosscutting issues within the NCA to identify sustainable and environmentally sound development pathways as part of a comprehensive assessment of global change impacts, adaptation, and vulnerability. Achieving this understanding requires coordinated development of future visions of climate, societal, and environmental conditions based on common assumptions and scientific information of assessment teams in regions and economic sectors. These scenarios are not intended to predict the future, but to better understand the implications of uncertainties in decision making. A common, coordinated suite of scenarios is useful, and can also provide input assumptions to various computer models that project forward in time to create possible future climate conditions. The NCA and the U.S. participation in the IPCC should facilitate the appropriate use of scenarios, technical guidelines, and tools to enable regional and sectoral analyses that are useful to stakeholders and scientists. Nested assessments within the centrally developed scenario-driven model outputs should also be supported to provide analysis at a variety of spatial scales. These assessments will help establish common bounding assumptions across the Nation, but do not preclude using alternative scenarios developed for more specific reasons.

A major challenge for scientific understanding and assessments generally is the strongly voiced need from policy makers for realistic projections at decision-relevant spatial and temporal scales. As the desired temporal and spatial scales shrink from long-term and global toward more local scales, some uncertainties in model output can increase and hence the information may be more difficult to interpret. Providing multiple timescale (e.g., seasonal to decadal) and spatial-scale information, while maintaining scientific rigor, is a strategic priority that will require significant effort over the coming decade (**Box 22**). It will also be crucial to clearly communicate the current status of uncertainties in understanding and in the modeling efforts. Over the next decade, USGCRP will coordinate closer integration across models of climate and global change and their impacts.

Increasingly, international collaborations on observations, scientific assessments, and model intercomparison projects are crucial components for understanding the U.S. context of climate change. Such collaborations synergistically enhance the capabilities of the U.S. science effort, and broaden the science basis for international assessments. For international assessments, USGCRP will continue to play a key role in leading, coordinating, and responding to international assessments, fostering U.S. participation and leadership in global efforts, such as the IPCC and the Arctic Climate Impact Assessment (**Box 33**). USGCRP will also support scientific involvement within the context of international collaborations that fulfill U.S. obligations to treaties such as the "Vienna Convention for the Protection of the Ozone Layer", and other assessments that are critical for efforts toward environmental treaty verification.

Box 32. Assessments to Improve Conservation Action

State, Federal, tribal, and nongovernmental organizations are responding to USGCRP findings on climate change and other landscape-scale changes, using them to identify opportunities for conservation and restoration at multiple scales. Nationwide, conservation organizations are partnering with government agencies on assessments to understand the combined impacts of climate change and other stressors, and to integrate that knowledge into conservation actions. Assessments, particularly when repeated or sustained, evaluate the effectiveness of the science, decision-support tools, approaches, and the progress they allow. Through its goal of "Conduct Sustained Assessments," USGCRP is creating a framework to enhance coordination and integration of various efforts across the country. The intent is to provide decision makers with authoritative information about natural resource management opportunities and constraints.

The right figure shows an example of a wildlife corridor. Such corridors allow wildlife to adapt to a multitude of stressors (such as during migration), including climate change. Interagency cooperation has led to assessment of existing corridors, and has facilitated effective placement of corridors.

Figure: This image illustrates why slower moving animals such as grizzly bears need alternative crossing paths provided by wildlife corridors. Image courtesy of Chuck Bartlebough.

Figure: A wildlife corridor. Image courtesy of Scott Jackson.

Objective 3.2: Ongoing Capacity

Strengthen and evolve ongoing capacity to conduct assessments with accessible, transparent, and consistent processes and broad participation of stakeholders across regions and sectors

Under USGCRP leadership, fostering an ongoing capacity to conduct assessments across the Nation requires the cooperation of a broad network of entities within and beyond USGCRP agencies. One approach to broad engagement is to establish and sustain a network of partners or "network of networks" that links and aligns Federal capacity with a wide range of interested communities. The intent is to partner with groups having both interest in climate and the capacity to provide support for the NCA and other assessments, such as governmental bodies (state, local, tribal), regional entities (e.g., governors' associations), nongovernmental organizations, trade associations, and academic institutions. The NCA intends to strengthen capacity to conduct assessments in a number of ways (e.g., training and technical assistance; partnerships with states, communities, nongovernmental organizations, and stakeholder groups) to improve institutional capability for, and commitment to, regular assessments.

Establishing a continuing, adaptive approach to national and international assessments starts with better coordination of Federal agency climate science, assessments, and services in each region and economic sector (**Box 30**). Many Federal agencies have regional offices and programs, with unique assets and capabilities, to actively engage with extensive networks of partners at local and regional scales, including partners in academia; state, local, and tribal governments; and the private sector. Harmonizing efforts within each region and providing benchmark scenarios of future conditions benefit both decision makers and information providers by avoiding duplication of efforts and leveraging existing capabilities. Coordination of these efforts must be founded on a commitment to sustained engagement and collaboration with public and private sector decision makers in a process of shared learning and joint problem-solving. It requires building a framework that provides effective regional and cross-regional coordination to meet the overall national needs, while preserving the necessary flexibility for enabling different approaches within any given region.

The Program will coordinate national assessment efforts across regions and sectors at multiple scales and build a sustained, collaborative network of public and private partners and stakeholders who are engaged in the NCA process. The National Climate Assessment Development and Advisory Committee, a Federal advisory committee responsible for producing the NCA reports, has been designed to foster the ongoing capacity of the assessment process and more fully engage all regions, sectors, and perspectives across the country. The Program will also use its international alliances to provide a valuable interface with international science, assessment, adaptation, and mitigation experience and promote improved access to information that supports global change information at multiple scales. Ultimately, the Federal effort should focus on supporting regional and international adaptation capacity, and thus extend beyond both the NCA and USGCRP.

Objective 3.3: Inform Responses

Inform responses to global change with accurate, authoritative, and timely information that is accessible to multiple audiences in multiple formats

Many decision makers, whether in government, nongovernmental organizations, or private industry, require information about global change. These audiences need scientific insights into the status, risks, and opportunities for adaptation and mitigation at a variety of scales, as well as the capacity to evaluate the utility of alternative approaches. A key role for USGCRP agencies is providing accurate, authoritative, and timely climate-related information, developed as part of Goal 1 (Advance Science) and Goal 2 (Inform Decisions), across the Nation and the world. Consistent scenarios of the future (Objective 3.1) provide a concrete example of this USGCRP role, and national indicators of global change will be developed to act as a benchmark across Federal to local planning efforts. The network designed to foster an ongoing capacity for assessment (Objective 3.2) must be intentionally designed to provide an information foundation so that best practices can be strengthened, needs identified, and tools developed to meet needs at all scales of decision making. These efforts will maximize equitable access to information that supports adaptation and mitigation decision making, especially for regions, sectors, ecosystems, populations, and systems (e.g., transportation, energy) that are identified as most vulnerable.

USGCRP will continue building rigorous processes to ensure the quality and transparency of data, information, and knowledge that are provided from the wide range of sources (see also Objectives 1.5 and 2.3). The network developed for ongoing capacity (Objective 3.2) will include not only traditional sources of information such as peer-reviewed literature but also other sources of useful information from state governments, businesses, or nongovernmental organizations, as well as indigenous knowledge from tribal sources. All of these sources will need to be evaluated prior to inclusion in assessment products with a consistent, clear, and objective procedure that not only exceeds the requirements of the Federal Information Quality Act, but also stands up to critical external appraisal.

It is critical for USGCRP to develop and deploy effective and efficient communications, outreach, education, and engagement processes including web-based data and tools and new media (e.g., social networking) to help make assessment information accessible and useful to the wide array of Program stakeholders. Successful implementation will include a national discourse on global change that involves scientists and other stakeholders and informs the public on climate and global change issues. Online access will increase the usefulness of the data and information collected for the assessments as well as support development of climate-related educational curricula. The development of a comprehensive and user-friendly website will be a critical component of the assessment, requiring a data architecture that supports robust archiving, retrieval, and quality assurance. Indeed, the needs of the NCA will be an initial test bed for development of a Federal interagency global change information system that will provide timely and relevant data and information to stakeholders, including the public (**Box 23**). Development of this information system will require close coordination with implementation of Goal 4 (Communicate and Educate).

Box 33. International Assessments

USGCRP and its member agencies coordinate a wide range of scientific participation in international assessments, where U.S. scientists play important roles in analyzing the current state of science and adaptation efforts worldwide. For instance, USGCRP coordinates participation of U.S. contributors to all IPCC working groups, and leads the process of author nominations and government and expert reviews of IPCC products, in cooperation with other Federal entities.

Another example of an important U.S. contribution coordinated through USGCRP was the development of the Arctic Climate Impact Assessment (ACIA). ACIA was an international project to evaluate and synthesize knowledge on climate variability, climate change, increased ultraviolet radiation, and their consequences. The United States is a member of the eight-nation Arctic Council, a high-level intergovernmental forum that requested this major assessment in response to clear evidence of major impacts on the Arctic and its people. Working with the International Arctic Science Committee, USGCRP agencies and U.S. scientists contributed to the activities necessary to bring this critical effort to fruition. The United States will chair the Arctic Council in 2015-2017, when significant activities, including the U.S.-chaired Sustained Arctic Observation Network, will be well underway. USGCRP will closely coordinate the Alaska regional assessment chapter of its 2017 NCA report with U.S. participation in these next pan-Arctic assessment and monitoring efforts.

Assessment Panels have been integral to the United Nation's Environment Programme's ozone protection regime since the very beginning of the implementation of the "Montreal Protocol on Substances that Deplete the Ozone Layer." Its panels for Technology and Economic Assessment, Scientific Assessment, and Environmental Effects Assessment have helped the parties to reach informed decisions and mitigation actions that have led to a reduction in the ozone hole. The United States, as one of the parties, relies on USGCRP science and observations to monitor the ozone layer, understand the contributions of naturally-occurring and human-induced processes to its variation, and provide predictive capability to study its future evolution in the context of changing distributions of industrially-produced source gases and a changing climate.

Figure: Cover page of the Fourth Assessment Report of the Intergovernmental Panel on Climate Change.

Figure: Cover page of the Arctic Climate Impacts Assessment.

Informing responses to global change requires ongoing evaluation of key issues for the Nation and evaluating progress toward reducing the Nation's vulnerability and risk. USGCRP, through the NCA process, will engage in designing and sustaining a small, coordinated suite of climate-related physical, ecological, and societal indicators that are easily communicated to interested parties (**Box 34**). They will be tracked as a part of ongoing, long-term assessment activities, with adjustments as necessary to adapt to changing conditions and understanding. These indicators offer the potential to provide:

- Meaningful climate-relevant information about the status and trends of key physical, ecological, and social variables and values to inform decisions on management, research, and education at regional to national scales, for key sectors identified by the NCA process

- An early warning of changes in climate-related conditions of selected resources and valued systems to help develop effective adaptation and mitigation measures and reduce costs of management

- Data to better understand the climate-driven dynamic nature and condition of Earth's systems and societies and to provide reference points for comparisons

The resulting national metrics will help decision makers understand progress being made in adapting to and mitigating climate change effects based on implemented policies and activities. The metric dashboard in **Box 34** is one concept to provide a user-friendly method to understand the cross-cutting indicators on a broad, comprehensive level. It also permits the user to focus on specific indicators that may contain information more applicable to their particular region of the country. By having this information easily accessible on a timely basis, decision makers around the Nation will be able to more quickly develop new ideas and practices to improve their ability to respond and adapt to climate change.

Box 34. Indicators of Global Change

The upper figure uses a "dashboard" to show how variations in indicators of global change can be summarized. Indicators reflect change over time in key variables, or in composites of several variables, that link climate and global change. Indicators often use time series records, such as the record of sea level variation shown in the lower right figure, which by themselves may not easily communicate usable information to decision makers. On the dashboard, warning lights appear along with a speedometer, and the lights turn on once their value exceeds a pre-determined threshold. The inverted triangle along the slider bar for each 'indicator' denotes the current status, while the colored vertical bar designates the threshold to turn the light 'on'. In this illustration, indicator C has reached a threshold and hence the light is yellow. The position of the speedometer along its track from 'favorable' to 'unfavorable' indicates the current status of the index comprising the four indicator metrics, and the position of the arrow, potentially from -180° to +180° captures the recent trend of the index over some period of time. Currently, the index is situated slightly past the 'favorable' status and the arrow indicates a trend continuing toward the right over the recent past.

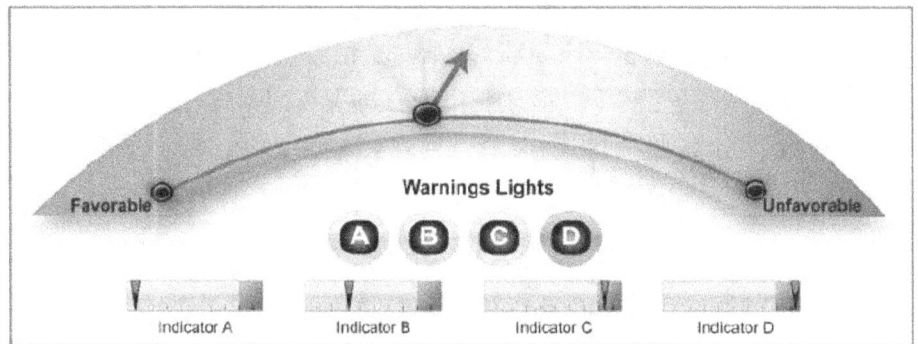

Dashboard showing variations in indicators of global change. Image courtesy of NCA Report Series Volume 5b "Monitoring Climate Change and its Impacts: Physical Climate Indicators."

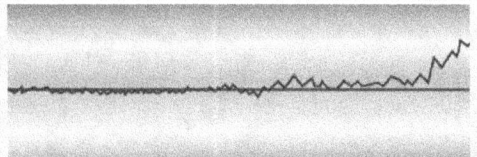

This illustration depicts the mock time series of one indicator ("C" in above figure). The colors denote whether this individual indicator has crossed from a favorable (green) status to a more negative one (yellow) and finally into an unfavorable zone (red).

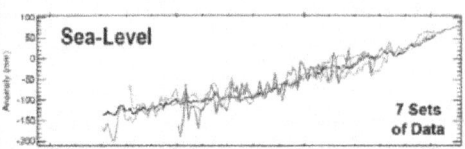

The record of changing sea level over time (taken from Box 20) is an example of the kind of information depicted to the left. In this example, the dashboard indicator might move towards the orange zone when the combination of observed sea level change and other variables indicate increased risk within a particular coastal management zone.

Objective 3.4: Evaluate Progress

Ensure ongoing evaluation of assessment processes and products, and incorporate the findings into an adaptive response for systemic improvement

A full evaluation of the national and international components of the USGCRP assessment process and products will be undertaken in an iterative fashion. Assessment products and processes to be evaluated are those mandated by the Global Change Research Act of 1990, including the relevant processes and products described in this USGCRP decadal strategy, and the U.S. contribution and participation in the IPCC. Evaluation of progress toward achieving the objectives of the NCA, and USGCRP participation in other assessments, will be institutionalized into the annual USGCRP work plan to support improvements in methodologies, process, and products of the assessments. The National Climate Assessment Development and Advisory Committee will continue to provide advice on the ongoing NCA processes. Finally, the National Research Council will be engaged to conduct an independent, external review of the NCA and USGCRP participation in other assessments.

Peer review of the assessment reports will involve academic, state, industry, international, and other groups conducting global change research. Criteria and metrics for peer review should include: scientific integrity of products and processes; the degree of integration, evaluation, and interpretation of findings; the scientific adequacy of analysis of global change effects; and transparency and credibility of data and sources evaluated within the context of the Federal information quality requirements.

Dialogue with actual and potential users of the results prior to, during, and upon completion of assessment processes and product development will ensure that such results are useful in developing policy responses to global change. Criteria could include, for example, evaluations of the degree to which products are used and useful by targeted stakeholders; a review of the "salience, credibility, and legitimacy" of products and processes; and measures of increases in end-user capacity.

Evaluation of participatory processes includes assessment of the quality, effectiveness, and sustainability of participation, and the extent of geographic and sectoral participation. The criteria for evaluation will in part consist of assessing how the various participation processes have contributed to the goals of the assessments. Other potential criteria for evaluating participation include assessing the breadth of representation in various activities, the nature of the relationships developed among the individuals and organizations that participate in NCA and other assessment activities, and the success in achieving the objectives and outcomes outlined in the NCA strategic plan. Progress toward building sustained assessment processes will come through a variety of formal and informal channels as part of a logical process that tracks participation from the time that an activity is initiated through the ultimate outputs, outcomes, impacts of the participation, and evaluation of the process and products. Each activity should include the opportunity for participants to provide feedback on their experience, minimally through a written evaluation, but also through mechanisms such as pre- and post-activity surveys of knowledge and capacity, more focused written or oral evaluations, and follow-up discussions with organizers.

Goal 4: Communicate and Educate

Advance communications and education to broaden public understanding of global change and develop the scientific workforce of the future

From communities, to businesses, to government agencies, global changes increasingly need to be considered when making decisions. A primary role of the USGCRP is to build a sound scientific foundation for global change knowledge, skill, and understanding that will support the Program's communication and education efforts. The Communicate and Educate goal will address public understanding and scientific workforce development. It will also complement efforts described in the Inform Decisions Goal.

The public is best served when connections between research outcomes and the things people care about (e.g., clean drinking water or shifts in their community's coastline) are clear and shown explicitly. Public surveys and assessments on the state of environmental literacy indicate that new approaches to communication and education efforts are needed to engage citizens in global change and related societal issues, such as energy and food security, and water availability.[13]

In the next decade, USGCRP will focus not only on fostering greater public understanding of the science through the dissemination of relevant, timely, and credible global change information, but also on gaining greater understanding of the public's science and information needs through engagement and dialogue. This two-pronged approach will help ensure decision makers at all levels have the capacity to make informed decisions and will be accomplished by the integration of communication, education, and engagement into core Program activities.

As the leading Federal authority on global change science, USGCRP, together with its member agencies, is uniquely positioned to serve as the gateway to global change information and will take a leadership role in the development of the scientific workforce of the future. Many Federal agencies have the capacity to communicate with citizens on specific aspects of global change, and they also have a long tradition in partnering and supporting higher education institutions in developing a pipeline of the scientific workforce relevant to global change. It is important, however, to recognize that one of the greatest strengths of USGCRP is its ability to develop synergies across Federal agencies in coordinating efforts in communication and education.

The USGCRP strategy for communication, education, and engagement efforts in the next decade will build on the strengths of the participating agencies. The Program will coordinate the development of multi-agency products and programs, grow and expand the reach of information beyond single agencies, and ensure that feedback and input from public engagement is shared broadly within the Federal global change science community.

USGCRP will accomplish its Communicate and Educate goal through four objectives that will be used to guide Program activities:

Objective 4.1 Strengthen Communication and Education Research: Strengthen the effectiveness of global change communication and education research to enhance practices

Objective 4.2 Reach Diverse Audiences: Enhance existing and employ emerging tools and resources to inform and educate effectively, providing for information flow in multiple directions

---

13. National Research Council. Informing an Effective Response to Climate Change. Washington, DC: The National Academies Press, 2010.

Objective 4.3 Increase Engagement: Establish effective and sustained engagement to enable a responsive and wholly integrated Program

Objective 4.4 Cultivate Scientific Workforce: Cultivate a capable, diverse scientific workforce that is knowledgeable about global change

The first three objectives address the need for broadening public awareness and understanding of global change through better awareness of citizens' existing knowledge and information needs. They also address the need to (1) employ a robust combination of tools and methods to effectively meet those needs, (2) build and sustain relationships to foster greater understanding of USGCRP programs and activities, and (3) develop methods and processes for engagement and dialogue. Objective 4.4 focuses on fostering an inter- or trans-disciplinary pathway beginning at the undergraduate level and the development of a highly capable, knowledgeable, and diverse scientific workforce that can meet the global change challenge.

Box 35. Building Climate Literacy

Climate literacy is knowledge and understanding of the concepts and processes that control Earth's climate; of the influence of climate on individuals, communities, and society; and of the influence of humans on climate. In partnership with scientific and educational organizations, USGCRP developed *Climate Literacy: The Essential Principles of Climate Science* (published in 2009). It continues to be used as a valuable resource for teachers, students, and community leaders as a basis for discussion within local communities, and as a guide for the development of informal learning resources and science curriculum content standards around the country.

Figure: High school students watch a demonstration at a "Science Careers in Search of Women" conference. Image courtesy of Argonne National Laboratory.

Figure: Cover of the report Climate Literacy: The Essential Principles of Climate Science, published in 2009 (for a copy, go to www.globalchange.gov/resources/educators/climate-literacy). Image courtesy of NOAA.

Objective 4.1: Strengthen Communication and Education Research

Strengthen the effectiveness of global change communication and education research to enhance practices

One of the key steps in ensuring the effective use of communication and education practices is to know the audience—what they already know, how they learn, and their preferred methods of communication. This knowledge will help convey clear and concise information through appropriate communication and education channels. The USGCRP will use knowledge gained from traditional research methods, such as observation, direct questions, surveys, and formal research, as a cornerstone in its communication and education efforts. It will further explore how knowledge production and shared learning can aid in enhancing communications and education activities.

Understanding the Audience

A major emphasis for USGCRP is to understand the connections among the environmental knowledge, opinions, attitudes, and behaviors of its diverse audiences. Such information will help USGCRP and its member agencies share scientific information effectively with the Program's different audiences, including Federal, state, local, and tribal organizations; local adaptation planners; scientists; businesses; students; and climate-interested citizens. Knowing the interests and background of the audiences is an important factor for communicating and educating effectively, as are the many important lessons that are provided by social science.[14] As USGCRP plans its communication, education, and engagement activities for the next 10 years, understanding the motivations, needs, and learning styles of diverse stakeholders will be central to developing tools and resources that are successful and widely used.

Research to Assess Global Change Education and Communication Effectiveness

Over the past decade, numerous agencies and institutions have invested in research on global change science knowledge, educational research, and communication. USGCRP and its member agencies will develop an understanding of what this research shows about the audiences and stakeholders the Program wants to reach, and identify priority areas where additional research is needed. Information gathered using a variety of research tools and methods, such as large-scale surveys, literature reviews, and listening sessions, will form the groundwork for prioritizing efforts. USGCRP will work with its member agencies to analyze the additional social science and education research that should be performed.

Establishing a global change information system (**Box 23**), assisting agency communications efforts using a variety of social media tools, and effectively coordinating national education programs are just a few areas where USGCRP research and coordinated communications activities can help the public understand options for shaping future directions. Developing global change science communicators and science storytellers, and creating a strategy for how best to communicate using new tools, are additional areas that research can strengthen.

---

14. National Research Council. *Informing an Effective Response to Climate Change*. Washington, DC: The National Academies Press, 2010.

Objective 4.2: Reach Diverse Audiences

Enhance existing and employ emerging tools and resources to inform and educate effectively, providing for information flow in multiple directions

Supporting research to understand audiences and gain insight into what sorts of tools and strategies will work to reach those audiences is only the first step in developing a strong communications and education program. USGCRP and its member agencies will develop, evaluate, and use effective methods and tools for translating global change science, and will provide these resources to those who need them.

Box 36. Science Learning

Learning is a life-long process. Museums, botanical gardens, zoos, aquariums, and libraries, as well as TV, the Internet, and other communications technologies help to generate awareness of, and interest in, the natural world. By taking advantage of these information resources, where new concepts may be introduced or others elaborated upon, people can increase their scientific understanding, and use it to enrich their interactions with the world around them.

USGCRP Federal agency members use informal environments for science learning, through activities such as developing community-educator partnerships and direct engagements with diverse audiences. For example, a resource package, *The Climate Change Wildlife and Wildlands Toolkit for Formal and Informal Educators*[15] was developed by multiple USGCRP agencies based on the award-winning and very popular toolkit first published in 2001. The updated 2007 toolkit includes an easy-to-

Figure: A citizen science backyard bird-banding program run by Smithsonian Migratory Bird Center. Image courtesy of Smithsonian Institution.

understand overview of the science of climate change, a DVD, classroom activities aligned with national science standards, and information on habitats and wildlife in 11 eco regions, as well as projects for kids.

Future directions for USGCRP informal education activities include contributing to:

- Museum exhibits and programs, including citizen science projects, to educate and engage citizens on the environmental changes happening around them
- Online resources for students and parents that include short presentations on a series of scientific topics, along with the opportunity to ask questions of scientists who are working for or with USGCRP agencies
- Resources and activities for K-16 or K-12 learners based on recent science findings that can be used in science-rich out-of-school settings by facilitators who know how to organize and support science learning

---

Optimize Human Interactions and Use of Technology

The fields of communications and education are changing, with new technologies for building social networks and interactivity reaching vast new audiences. The USGCRP of the next decade will need to adopt many existing technological advances, as well as embrace emerging ones, to provide global change educational information and communications. Social media will play a growing role in USGCRP communications activities, and communicators and educators within the Program will work to develop other new media tools that can engage the public in global change science. With its coordination role among the Federal agencies, USGCRP has the advantage of being able to combine and build upon

---

15. For more information, go to http://www.globalchange.gov/resources/educators/toolkit

the existing skills and considerable technological capacities of individual agencies to cooperate in devising cutting-edge communication and education tools. In addition, USGCRP will promote people-driven capabilities, such as agency extension services and community-based outreach, to reach a more diverse audience. And above all, flexibility will be important for developing the most relevant, usable, and timely resources. USGCRP communications and education should remain up-to-date and include adaptability to emerging technologies as a main component of its efforts, including the evaluation of their effectiveness.

Support Forums for Dialogue

Communications tools are not limited to technological resources, but also include resources that define new ways of communicating and educating. As such, an important component of USGCRP communication and education will be developing communities of practice, where experts will have the opportunity to discuss projects that have the potential to span agencies and scientific specialty fields and leverage skills that exist within each agency for the benefit of the greater whole. USGCRP will support Federal interagency groups that function as communities of practice, bringing together diverse education, communication, public information, extension services, engagement, and new media experts to share research findings, tools, and practices, and work together to develop interagency projects.

Promote Interdisciplinary Learning

Essential to the USGCRP mission is the improvement of the scientific accuracy, educational effectiveness, and usability of communication and education materials and resources. These resources must incorporate an integrated Earth system science approach, social science, and educational research findings, and promote an interdisciplinary framework. USGCRP will leverage its partnerships to convey timely curriculum materials and scientific content to higher education organizations and others who teach about global climate change. Through productive workshops (**Box 35**), USGCRP partners and collaborators have begun to develop interdisciplinary learning resources that connect education and communications practices with science content that addresses Earth climate, impacts of climate change, and approaches to adaptation or mitigation using a climate literacy framework. Collaboration with state and local entities ensures that the materials will have validity and usability for diverse communities. USGCRP will coordinate its efforts with other education initiatives at USGCRP agencies to provide opportunities for educators and learners to actively integrate across the diverse disciplines of global change science, including social sciences such as economics and sociology.

Further, USGCRP and its member agencies will provide the knowledge base for informal science learning programs at zoos, botanical parks, arboretums, museums, aquariums, and similar institutions. Such informal settings provide ideal opportunities to citizens of all ages and backgrounds to explore ways in which global change is affecting local communities. USGCRP research will be extended to enrich programs that allow citizens, including children in elementary schools, to learn foundational knowledge about global change science research. With an appropriately forward-looking approach, global change education and communication efforts within USGCRP agencies will serve the broader need to invest in the next generation of scientists, engineers, and educators so the Nation can remain at the forefront of innovation and competition in the 21st century global marketplace.

Objective 4.3: Increase Engagement

Establish effective and sustained engagement to enable a responsive and wholly integrated Program

Effective engagement with a person, group, or organization requires a dialogue to better discern needs, issues, understanding, and expectations. Transparency and openness in communication and education builds credibility and trust. USGCRP will engage a broad array of stakeholders, both within the United States and internationally, to ensure that Federal science is effective in addressing their issues and needs. The Program is uniquely positioned to broaden and expand existing relationships with stakeholders as well as forge new relationships through the extension of participating Federal agencies. This activity will be done in coordination with and in support of Goal 2 (Inform Decisions).

Build and Maintain Relationships

USGCRP will develop programs and forms of engagement to facilitate communication and education among citizens, stakeholders, partners, and the participating agencies. Providing timely, reliable, and credible information products and services to these audiences, which are relevant and easy to use, will lead to establishing long-lasting relationships. Providing these products is important across the Program and in the context of the NCA.

Tailoring engagement methods to stakeholders' needs supports effective engagement, and positive outcomes. Working with partners, USGCRP and its agencies will use current knowledge of audiences, including understanding of their interests, motivations, and needs as related to global change science (Objective 4.1) to develop effective engagement tools and technologies (Objective 4.2). USGCRP will seek input and feedback from partners, participating agencies, and constituents. Engagement activities will create pathways for public feedback and information needs that will be considered during the annual development of science priorities (Goal 1: Advance Science), help guide development of more effective decisions, and enhance assessment activities (Goal 2: Inform Decisions and Goal 3: Conduct Sustained Assessments).

Box 37. Global Change in Your Backyard

Phenology is a scientific term for the timing of activity of plants and animals, such as the appearance each year of leaves and flowers, maturation of crops, emergence of insects, laying of eggs, timing of hibernations, and the migrations of birds. Knowledge of phenology is critical for helping farmers and gardeners know when to plant or harvest, helping environmental managers anticipate drought and wildfire risks, and helping public health officials predict allergy season or the spread of mosquito-borne diseases. Phenology is nature's calendar.

Changes in phenology are among the most sensitive biological indicators of global change. Across the world, many springtime events are occurring earlier—and fall events happening later—than in the past. These changes are happening quickly for some species and more slowly, or not at all, for others, altering relationships and processes that have been stable for thousands of years. Scientists need more and better information about the pace and patterns of these changes to answer important scientific questions and to build the tools and models needed to help people understand and adapt to the changes.

USA-NPN Observation Sites

Figure: Map of the U.S. showing the locations of the National Phenology Networks Observer Stations. Image courtesy of the National Phenology Network.

The USA National Phenology Network (USA-NPN) monitors the phenology of plants, animals, and landscapes and provides key data to uncover trends and changes on a national scale. USA-NPN is a partnership among governmental and nongovernmental science and resource management agencies and organizations, the academic community, and the public. These groups and institutions work together to collect and organize species and timing information to inform research, education and outreach, agriculture, tourism and recreation, human health, and natural resource conservation and management. USA-NPN encourages people of all ages and backgrounds to observe phenological events as a way to discover and explore the world. By providing a place for people to enter, store, and share their observations, it also makes it possible for the public to help researchers improve understanding about how changes in phenology relate to climate change.

USA-NPN activities—which are supported by a number of USGCRP agencies—are organized through its National Coordinating Office at the University of Arizona. Support for organizations like USA-NPN is critical to engage even more members of the public in the scientific enterprise and make it easier for their observations to become part of the large body of Earth system data used by researchers, farmers, government officials, and businesses. Harnessing new technologies, such as applications for mobile devices and social networking sites, will be essential for future progress. Overall, increasing public involvement in the process of science, including data collection, analysis, and interpretation, will strengthen the national global change research enterprise and increase public literacy in global change science.

Figure: Citizen scientist observing the phenology of a bristly locust (Robinia hispida) in Concord, Massachusetts. Image courtesy of Richard Primack and Abraham Miller-Rushing.

Develop Methods and Processes

USGCRP and its member agencies will increase understanding of information pathways and channels by conducting audience analyses to learn how audiences create, receive, and use information. The Program will expand its reach by leveraging existing communications and engagement channels established by the member Federal agencies. USGCRP will use collaboration technologies, such as tools that help people share different perspectives, collaborate across disciplines, and facilitate the creative process. The development of both virtual and actual communities of practice will provide the opportunity for communication and education professionals to network and identify counterparts and partners as well as to share knowledge and best practices.

Objective 4.4: Cultivate Scientific Workforce

Cultivate a capable, diverse scientific workforce that is knowledgeable about global change

Underpinning the success of the broad and ambitious research agenda laid out in this Plan is a highly capable and skilled scientific workforce. These future leaders in global change research will help the U.S. respond to the multiple stresses experienced in all dimensions of global change within and beyond its shores. The accomplishments that USGCRP has made over the past two decades in interdisciplinary integration, particularly in climate science, points to the strategic direction of a more meaningful collaboration and integration with social and economic sciences. Further, USGCRP will continue a deeper integration of all components of the Earth system science needed to support U.S. and international assessments and risk management. This must start with undergraduate teaching and research, and continuing through graduate and postdoctoral levels.

Across universities and colleges in the U.S., there have been many examples of inter- or trans-disciplinary programs bringing together the intellectual expertise from physical, chemical, and biological disciplines as well as the humanities, ranging from geography, anthropology, and economics to political and behavioral sciences. Many presidents of these universities and colleges have also pledged to exercise leadership in the academic communities in integrating sustainability into the curriculum.[16] A true diversity in the science workforce, from gender, racial, ethnic, cultural, to physical conditions, must also start at universities and colleges.

To ensure U.S. leadership in science and technology, USGCRP and its member agencies will continue to invest and leverage their partnerships with universities and colleges in developing the pathway for a highly capable, knowledgeable, and diverse scientific workforce to meet the global change challenge. Particular emphasis will be on the integration of the socio-economic with the physical, chemical, and biological sciences that starts at the undergraduate level and continues through graduate education, postdoctoral programs, and the research enterprise spanning the Federal, academic and industrial sectors.

---

16. For more information, visit http://www.presidentsclimatecommitment.org/

Box 38. The Changing Carbon Cycle: Understanding Human Influences on Climate Change

Carbon is continually cycled throughout the Earth system. Living organisms exhale, digest, and decompose carbon compounds. The oceans absorb carbon dioxide, freshwater and marine organisms take it in as they grow. This process of carbon transformation, storage, and eventual release back into the atmosphere is part of "the carbon cycle."

Humans, however, have upset the overall balance of this cycle, mainly via fossil fuel combustion and land-use changes, such as deforestation, which release previously stored carbon as carbon dioxide and methane, thus increasing the concentrations of these greenhouse gases in the atmosphere. These human-induced changes create a greenhouse effect that will have cascading impacts on climatic, biological, and oceanic processes for hundreds to thousands of years. For example, oceanic uptake of carbon increases the acidity of the oceans, negatively impacting much of their biodiversity. The overall impact on the Earth system of these changes to the carbon cycle depends in part on complex interactions with the water cycle and other elements, such as nitrogen, phosphorus, sulfur, and calcium. It also depends strongly on many components of human systems, including agriculture, demographics, culture, water and energy use, and security.

The carbon cycle cuts across many disciplines and is central to three major global change issues: impacts of global change that could accelerate increases in atmospheric greenhouse gas concentrations, such as thawing of permafrost and release from ocean sediments; societal actions that will affect the amounts of greenhouse gases in the atmosphere; and direct effects of carbon dioxide increases that are independent of climate change, such as ocean acidification (**Box 10**) and effects on terrestrial ecosystems.

Carbon Cycle Strategic Planning

Several documents developed by the multi-disciplinary carbon cycle science community have served as key sources for USGCRP-sponsored carbon cycle research, assessment, decision-support, outreach, and communication. In 1999, the carbon cycle science community developed a science plan that led to the development of two major programs – the North American Carbon Program (NACP) and the Ocean Carbon and Biogeochemistry Program (OCB). Together, these programs developed a strategy for observations, process research, and modeling to diagnose the balance of carbon sources and sinks on land and in the ocean, to understand the processes that control these flows, and to provide the scientific basis for societal responses to global change, such as carbon sequestration. In 2011, a new decadal carbon cycle science plan was published in response to evolving societal needs. It calls for increased attention to the effect of humans on the carbon cycle and the need to integrate social sciences into carbon cycle science research, including socio-demographic, socio-economic, and socio-political causes of variability in carbon emissions and the consequences of carbon mitigation and climate adaptation strategies.

Maintaining Core Observations

Observing systems and networks that measure the atmosphere, ocean, terrestrial ecosystems, and human activities are integral parts of carbon cycle science and need to be expanded and sustained. Data from sampling programs, tower networks, *in situ* observations, and remote sensing from planes, ocean platforms, and satellites are essential to process understanding and modeling efforts. They document changes in concentrations and flows of atmospheric greenhouse gases, carbon dioxide concentrations in oceans, carbon in soils, use of forests and natural resources, ecosystem productivity and health, impacts of land-use change, and numerous societal parameters. The NACP and OCB programs promote long-term accessibility of these data through data centers and policies maintained by participating agencies.

Conducting Process Research

Process research provides a mechanistic understanding of drivers and feedbacks to the global carbon cycle. Research over the last 20 years has increased the awareness of carbon cycle processes and effects of rising carbon dioxide and temperatures in both managed and unmanaged ecosystems and over geologic time. For example, scientists now better understand the limits and variability of the effects of carbon dioxide fertilization, including the potential for enhanced decomposition of soil carbon, the processes influencing carbon dioxide uptake in a warming ocean, and the consequences of the interplay between management and climate-induced stress on forests, crops, and pests. Studies of natural or human-induced disturbances, such as fire, thawing permafrost, melting sea ice, water deficits and management, and land use, have increased our understanding of geographic and ecosystem differences in carbon vulnerabilities to change and disturbance. Important components of this research are intensive, inter-agency coordinated field studies that allow us to bring resources of all agencies to bear on the relative influences of human and natural processes on carbon cycle variability and change.

Figure: The two major emission sources: fossil fuel burning and land use change. (top) Figure: Coal power plant along the Patapsco River, Baltimore MD. Image courtesy of Joanna Woerner, Integration and Application Network, University of Maryland Center for Environmental Science (http://ian.umces.edu/imagelibrary/). (bottom) A cleared forest in Brazil. Image courtesy of Compton Tucker.

Figure: Scientists conducting an Ameriflux comparison at Sky Oaks Field Station. Image courtesy of the Field Stations Program, College of Sciences at San Diego State University http://fs.sdsu.edu/.

17. Pan, Y, et al., 2011. A Large and Persistent Carbon Sink in the World's Forests. Science, 333. DOI: 10.1126/science.1201609.

18. For more information about Surface Ocean CO2 Variability and Vulnerability, visit http://www.socat.info/about.html.

19. North American Carbon Program (CarboNA) science plan, for more information on the North American Carbon Program, visit http://nacarbon.org/carbona/carbona_science_plan.htm.

Modeling

Incorporating improved carbon models into climate and Earth system models is critical for increasing accuracy and reducing uncertainties of predictions. For example, the Multi-scale Synthesis and Terrestrial Model Intercomparison Project provides feedback to improve the diagnosis and attribution of carbon sources and sinks through an integrated framework of models and observations. CarbonTracker, another example, uses high-accuracy atmospheric measurements to constrain fluxes derived from land and ocean models and graphically displays atmospheric greenhouse gases around the globe.

Decision Support and Outreach

Several decision support and outreach tools are under development: an online tool that assesses carbon sequestration and greenhouse gas implications of land management practices; forest management training to reduce vulnerability to climate-induced pest outbreaks; and extension programs to increase soil carbon sequestration in cropping systems. Also, national and international assessments use scientific data to inform policy-makers and society. For example, USGCRP's carbon cycle research is used extensively in IPCC assessments and annual state of the climate reports. American scientists also recently published the first State of the Carbon Cycle Report.

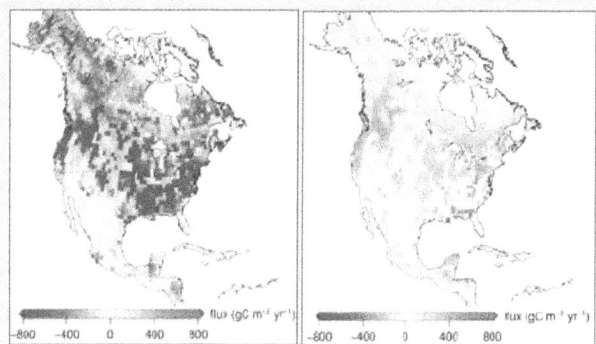

Figure: Carbon fluxes to the atmosphere from North American ecosystems for June (L) and December (R) 2009, as determined by CarbonTracker. A negative flux (blue) means a net uptake of CO2 from the atmosphere. These figures do not include emissions from fossil fuel burning. Image courtesy of NOAA.

International Coordination

USGCRP's Carbon Cycle Science Program (CCSP), a partner in the international Global Carbon Project (GCP), engages the GEO-Carbon community of practice. It contributes to the Global Climate Observation System and its terrestrial and oceanic components, Global Terrestrial Observing System and Global Ocean Observing System, and co-leads the Committee on Earth Observing Satellites. The CCSP participates actively in GCP's Regional Carbon Cycle Assessment and Processes, contributed two recent assessments of the global forest carbon sink[17], and contributes to the surface ocean CO2 atlas.[18] Another key international partnership is CarboNA,[19] a collaboration among Canada, Mexico, and the United States for carbon cycle science research throughout North America and adjacent coastal waters. In the United States, CarboNA includes work from both the NACP and the OCB programs with several joint international projects under development with a focus on emphasis areas that require or take advantage of cross-border collaboration.

The Way Forward

Over the next decade, USGCRP will foster the comprehensive research needed to gain further understanding of the changing carbon cycle, most importantly to better understand the direct and indirect influence of human activities, and to assess the potential for climate-induced feedbacks that could lead to the release of additional stored carbon as greenhouse gases. Building on the existing framework and partnerships, USGCRP will seek to enhance engagement of social scientists and potential users of this information and will continue to provide a critical knowledge base for informed decision making and action in the face of global change.

Figure: Covers of publications that USGCRP published or contributed to their publication.

Cover from A U.S. Carbon Cycle Science Plan, produced by the USGCRP Carbon Cycle Science Program, lead authors Anna M. Michalak, Robert B. Jackson, Gregg Marland, and Christopher Sabine

IV. International Cooperation

Global change is at its core an issue that requires an international, coordinated response. Effectively advancing the understanding of global change, establishing and sustaining observations, and preparing for global environmental change require concerted international cooperation and collaboration. Because of a mandate that spans from coordinating basic research to communicating and informing the response, it is important for USGCRP to engage with other nations and international organizations.

The U.S. Congress recognized the importance of international cooperation and collaboration and codified it in the Global Change Research Act. USGCRP is mandated, in the Act of 1990, to: (1) coordinate U.S. activities with other nations and international organizations on global change research projects and activities, (2) promote international cooperation and access to scientific data and information, and (3) participate in international global change research by developing nations. Through international engagement, USGCRP and its member agencies can effectively leverage existing and future scientific capabilities to more effectively use resources to accomplish goals and strategic priorities.

The international activities that USGCRP supports, and collectively participates in, have resulted in substantially improved understanding of the Earth system processes that underlie global change. They have provided scientific results and data that have improved models of global change and scenarios that predict such change and its impact. These activities have made major contributions to the work of the IPCC. USGCRP also plays a vital coordinating role in international scientific assessments (**Box 33**). These programs and their associated infrastructure provide an essential framework within which U.S. scientists lead, conduct, and participate in a wide range of international global change research projects that advance key scientific objectives of the USGCRP. These global efforts have provided the U.S. science community with opportunities to develop long-term collaborative partnerships with international colleagues.

Using the collective knowledge and expertise across its participating Federal agencies, USGCRP is uniquely positioned to identify potential synergies with international organizations and pursue collaborative programs that bridge the environmental and societal challenges faced by governments, businesses, communities, and society. By leveraging international knowledge, USGCRP can achieve a global change research program that will support delivery of knowledge and data that advances science, informs adaptation and mitigation decisions, sustains assessments, and strengthens communication and education. To achieve this vision of integrated and societally relevant research, USGCRP engages with a variety of international programs such as the World Climate Research Programme (WCRP), the International Geosphere-Biosphere Program (IGBP), the International Human Dimensions Program (IHDP), the Earth Systems Science Partnership (ESSP), DIVERSITAS[20], and the SysTem for Analysis, Research

---

20. An International Programme of Biodiversity Science (also the Latin word for "biodiversity")

and Training (START). USGCRP also supports regional activities through the Inter-American Institute for Global Change Research (IAI), the Asia-Pacific Network for Global Change Research (APN), and the African Network for Earth System Science (AfricanNESS). Individual USGCRP agencies provide additional support to other programs and projects that advance collaborative multidisciplinary research relevant to global environmental change, and its impacts on society. These types of global partnerships maximize international scientific exchange and best practices, support complementary research efforts, and allow decision makers to make more informed science-based decisions domestically and globally.

As domestic global change policy requires closer connections between the physical and biological sciences, and the social and behavioral sciences, so too will international global change policy. While the natural sciences provide insight into how the environment may change, the social sciences are needed to provide the critical information about how people and societies may behave in the face of change and how societal values may influence and respond to policy decisions. Given that such values and behavior may vary from one country to the next, and even within countries, it is important that the global dimensions of the social sciences relevant to the relationship with the environment are understood, and this can only be done through international cooperation.

The mission of the USGCRP aligns with efforts being undertaken by the international community, in which the traditional physical and biological research focus on global change is being restructured to respond to the growing demand for information and products by both the public and private sectors. The International Council for Science (ICSU), with the International Social Science Council (ISSC) and other partners, including the Belmont Forum, is shaping the future of international global change research coordination (**Box 39**). Another example of

---

Box 39. New Directions in International Cooperation

Understanding and responding to environmental change at global and regional levels requires greater scientific expertise, technological capabilities, and resources than any one country can manage alone. Congress recognized the need for international cooperation at the outset of the USGCRP.

The international scientific community has recognized the need for a new unifying vision to coordinate global change research at the international level. The leadership of the ICSU, with input from USGCRP, is shaping the development of an international vision with support and contributions by agencies that fund global environmental change research. The Belmont Forum and the International Group of Funding Agencies for Global Change Research (IGFA) are working with ICSU and the ISSC to expand the requirements needed to understand global and regional change and to apply that knowledge for societal benefit.

In parallel, long-standing international organizations such as the World Meteorological Organization (WMO), the United Nations Environment Programme (UNEP), and the Consultative Group on International Agricultural Research (CGIAR) system, are restructuring their organizations to develop new programs that address climate and global change. Best available scientific practices and observations at local and regional scales are essential for these organizations to successfully deliver information to end users and decision makers globally.

Although the United States and other major industrialized countries currently conduct the majority of research on climate and global change, understanding such change on global and regional scales requires scientific information and observations from regions of the globe where scientific capabilities are not as well developed. It will be necessary to work with international funding agencies, private sector and non-profit entities to help the countries in these regions, their scientists, and their institutions build capabilities and knowledge that will enable them to contribute to regional and global programs.

efforts to advance cooperation among international global environmental change communities can be found in the outcomes of the World Climate Conference-3[21], with a decision to establish a Global Framework for Climate Services (GFCS) to strengthen the application of science-based climate prediction and services around the world. Such a framework could be tremendously valuable in managing global climate-related risks by maximizing the existing global investments in observing, monitoring, and modeling systems, and providing global change information. It also has the potential to offer significant economic, public health and safety, and security benefits for participating countries. The physical, biological, and social science research that is being undertaken in USGCRP agencies is highly relevant to the GFCS. USGCRP is already working with WCRP to develop the modeling and understanding components of the GFCS that will emphasize linkages to adaptation and observations. USGCRP can further contribute to, and benefit from, this emerging framework through increased coordination with the international community to provide global change information.

Enhancing cooperation between the international community and USGCRP promotes scientific diplomacy, in which scientific partnerships serve as catalysts for building relationships with other countries. The provision of data and other scientific outputs to other countries can help support global sustainable development, and complement U.S. initiatives in policy and security. USGCRP coordination of global change information, as discussed in **Box 23,** can inform more robust decisions related to U.S. international development efforts, such as those being made in response to the Presidential Policy Directive on Global Development, including areas such as climate change, food security and health. USGCRP science is also used to inform U.S. positions in a variety of international bodies.

Sustained global observing systems are essential to global change research and require international partnerships. *In situ* and satellite-based observations of the environment are of fundamental

---

Box 40. Collaborative Data Collection

Many U.S. global change observing systems benefited greatly from highly substantive international collaborations. Some illustrations provide a view of the important role played by other countries. Each example describes acquisition of data critical to achieving the USGCRP Vision.

- NASA and the French space agency Centre National d'Etudes Spaciales (CNES) designed, built, and launched three research satellite missions to establish a 20-year stable, highly accurate, and well-calibrated global sea level time series. It is now operated by NOAA, in the United States, and the European Organisation for the Exploitation of Meteorological Satellites (EUMETSAT). A fourth satellite mission to continue the sea level record is being planned.

- NASA worked with international partners in the design of its Earth Observing System. For example, the Netherland's Ozone Monitoring Instrument (OMI), which includes contributions from Finland, flies on NASA's Aura satellite, and Japan's Advanced Spaceborne Thermal Emission and Reflector Radiometer (ASTER) instrument is on NASA's Terra satellite.

- The NASA Aquarius sea surface salinity instrument was launched in June 2011 on an Argentine satellite.

- *In situ* observing systems have benefited through international collaboration. U.S. agencies depended on international investments in the 3,000-element free-floating Argo float array to deploy U.S. floats and to contribute additional floats.

- Data integration initiatives, such as the Global Biodiversity Information Facility (GBIF), bring data from disparate sources together for use by scientists and citizens.

---

21. World Climate Conference -3 2009; http://www.wmo.int/wcc3/page_en.php

importance to understanding the Earth system. Because these observations are of great value globally, require significant investments of resources, and need to be collected outside of the United States, international partnerships are crucial to leverage investments, expand system coverage and increase useable science. The global scientific community has recognized the value of intelligently connected and consistent observing systems that incorporate both longer term (sustained) and shorter term (intensive) observations. These systems ultimately need to be transparent in several aspects including calibration, algorithms, and data utilization; collected data should be shared fully and openly. An international effort to modernize historical data for use in today's research is also vital. Such systems could increase compatibility between data from different sources, significantly improve and advance understanding of change, and better inform responses at global, regional, national, and even subnational scales.

Continued engagement with international partners on *in situ* global change monitoring networks, including deployment of equipment within partner borders, will result in more extensive geographical coverage of observations, and will also provide critical calibration and validation of satellite measurements and gathering of complementary data. Focused, process-oriented field campaigns depend upon the joint effort of multiple countries to ensure consistent and comprehensive data collection. To ensure coordination among efforts by Federal agencies, USGCRP works with entities such as the U.S. Group on Earth Observations and the Interagency Working Group on Digital Data; both help set the standards and coordination of Earth observation data in a long-term, durable, and usable fashion.

Global change research requires observations of more than climate and other environmental factors. It also requires social and behavioral science observations and measurements such as census data and economic impact information. Acquiring these measurements requires close collaboration between USGCRP and other international organizations, and increasingly with the private sector.

Global change poses difficult problems that will require a coordinated global effort for understanding and response. Decades of experience have shown that progress is more rapid if nations combine their intellectual, scientific and observing resources and assets. Through international partnerships, USGCRP can leverage the best-available science and practices from around the world to inform U.S. policy and program decisions, and ultimately advance understanding of, and responses to, global change.

Box 41. Past Climate Informs Future Decisions

Earth's climate is changing rapidly with unknown consequences for ecosystems and society. Atmospheric greenhouse gas concentrations, including carbon dioxide, have risen to levels not recorded for at least 3 million years. Oceans are becoming more acidic due to the uptake of carbon dioxide from the atmosphere. Atmospheric and ocean temperatures are increasing, Arctic sea-ice cover is decreasing, and glaciers and parts of the Greenland and Antarctic ice sheets are melting, contributing to rising sea level. Changes in precipitation are resulting in extreme droughts and floods in many regions, affecting crops, fisheries and other commercial activities. Because records of rainfall and temperature cover only a century or so of Earth's 4 5 billion year history, it is necessary to study past climate changes using the geological record to provide a baseline to evaluate recent changes and improve the understanding of likely impacts of future climate change. Data on climates of the distant past can also be useful as tests of models used to project future climate.

A global, interdisciplinary effort in paleoclimatology, the study of past climates, has made major scientific discoveries directly relevant to today's climate challenges. There is now unequivocal evidence that Earth's climate changes occur over timescales ranging from decades to millions of years due to many factors, including greenhouse gas concentrations, solar output, volcanic activity, cycles in the Earth-sun orbit, the position of the continents, ocean circulation, and interactions among the atmosphere, oceans, land surfaces, glaciers, and ice sheets. Paleoclimate research documents past responses of the Earth system to climate extremes and abrupt changes, providing key insights into potential rates of change, tipping points, and effects on ecosystems.

Figure: The Taxodium (cypress) pollen grain shown above was recovered from sediments deposited in the Arctic Ocean (star in map above) during the Paleocene-Eocene Thermal Maximum, approximately 55 million years ago. Pollen and other fossils provide a means to reconstruct past patterns of temperature, precipitation, atmospheric carbon dioxide concentration, and other environmental parameters. Cypress forests, such as the one illustrated in the figure, now occur only as far north as New York state, and the occurrence of cypress pollen near the modern North Pole illustrates the potential shifts of biota under different climate conditions. Image courtesy of USGS and Utrecht University.

Cycles of natural climate variability occur over timescales ranging from years to millions of years, and a comprehensive understanding of these processes requires research on timescales ranging from "deep time" (tens of millions of years or more) to the current interglacial period that covers the last ~11,000 years. For example, research shows that Earth's climate is dominated by quasi-periodic glacial-interglacial (ice age) cycles caused by changes in the Earth's orbital geometry relative to the sun, changing the seasonal and geographic distribution of the sun's energy. These orbital climate changes (Milankovitch cycles) are characterized by fluctuations in global temperature, sea level, and the global carbon cycle. Warm climate extremes, known as hyperthermal events, also punctuate Earth history and provide evidence of the Earth system response to increased atmospheric carbon dioxide concentrations. One such event, the Paleocene Eocene Thermal Maximum (PETM) 55 million years ago, had a global temperature spike of 6°C (11°F) in 20,000 years, caused at least in part by increased carbon dioxide concentrations. Paleoclimate records of natural carbon dioxide fluctuations and ecosystem responses provide decision makers with direct information about the fate of human fossil fuel carbon emissions, and the Earth's climate sensitivity to future increased carbon dioxide concentrations.

Another key research theme involves the threat of abrupt climate change, which is a major concern to agriculture, commerce, coastal regions, national security, energy policy, and more. Abrupt changes in climate, occurring over only decades to centuries, are common in the paleoclimate record and provide analogs to evaluate whether Earth is now experiencing an abrupt climate transition. Two examples of abrupt climate transitions that would significantly affect society include rapid sea-level rise and altered patterns of drought and extreme flooding. Paleoclimate records from the last deglaciation from 18,000 to 10,000 years ago show that ice-sheet collapse caused rapid sea-level rise, changes in climate, and altered ocean circulation. Such records are key to improving predictions about the rate of future sea-level rise due to melting of parts of the Greenland and Antarctic ice sheets.

Severe drought in the western United States since 1999 highlights the need to assess to what degree this drought and those of the 1930s "Dust Bowl" and 1950s reflect human-induced changes and whether rainfall extremes can be expected in the future. Tree-ring, sediment, coral and mineral deposits formed in caves serve as "proxy" records of rainfall from North America for the past millennium. They show that decade-long regional and continental-scale droughts are an inherent feature of Earth's climate, especially during the 11th through 14th centuries. The severity of droughts varied greatly across regions of the U.S., but clearly affected western Native American societies such as the Pueblo and Anasazi. It is not yet possible to predict the effect of future greenhouse gas increases on North American droughts; however, it is clear that a return to medieval-type droughts would significantly increase water scarcity in the western U.S.

In addition to reconstruction of natural climate variability, paleoclimate studies inform decision makers about the degree to which human activities such as carbon emissions and land use changes have altered climate. One specific application involves international efforts to distinguish human-induced climate change, due to increased carbon emissions and land use change, from those driven by solar activity, volcanic emissions, and other factors. Integrated research efforts based on 2000-year long paleoclimate reconstructions from tree rings, ice cores, marine and terrestrial sediments, glaciers, and instrumental records have been combined with climate modeling to sort out natural climate processes from those related to human activity. Additional applications use paleoreconstructions of the ocean carbonate system to understand how climate influences the biogeochemical cycles associated with ocean acidification and effects on organisms. Calcite and aragonite levels in the ocean fluctuate with atmospheric carbon dioxide concentrations, and paleoclimate proxies can provide critical records documenting pH variability response to natural climate variability and greenhouse gases.

In sum, today's climate is experiencing unprecedented changes on a scale seen only in the geological record of past climate changes. Paleoclimate reconstructions are informing decisions about mitigation response to regional rainfall extremes, management and engineering in low-lying coastal regions, energy development, water management and agriculture, international security, commercial and transportation in polar regions, and managing threatened species and ecosystems. Such information provides the foundation to understand climate impacts across society and to improve climate predictions of future climate change.

V. Implementation Strategy

This decadal Strategic Plan builds upon USGCRP accomplishments to further strengthen scientific understanding of global change. It also lays out a program that will more effectively translate this scientific understanding into information that society can use for decision making. It articulates the Program's research goals, provides a framework for informing decisions and assessing progress, and outlines interagency capabilities and needs to support future activities.

The USGCRP is committed to implementing this Strategic Plan, but realistic about the challenges, particularly in a constrained budget environment. These include, but are not limited to: (1) the need to foster further development of the highest quality science within the Program's mandate, including biological and human impact research; (2) the need to establish USGCRP priorities on timescales shorter than this decadal plan that deliver essential capabilities and foster collaborations and partnerships to achieve the Strategic Plan; and (3) the need to align fundamental and use-inspired research to maximize the impact from USGCRP investments in policy and application.

Governance and Program Coordination

The Subcommittee on Global Change Research (SGCR) plans and coordinates the USGCRP. The SGCR reports to the National Science and Technology Council's Committee on Environment, Natural Resources, and Sustainability, which is administered by the White House Office of Science and Technology Policy (OSTP) on behalf of the Assistant to the President for Science and Technology (**Box 6**). The SGCR is composed of representatives from each of the thirteen participating agencies and departments (denoted as "The Principals"), and is led by a Chair from one of the participating agencies. The SGCR also has representation from OSTP, Office of Management and Budget (OMB), and CEQ. The SGCR has responsibility for setting strategic direction and priorities for the USGCRP and overseeing their implementation. The Executive Director – a Federal employee serving under the authority of an NSTC detail to the White House Office of Science and Technology Policy (OSTP)[22] – is responsible for overseeing integration and planning activities of the USGCRP and the implementation of interagency efforts on behalf of the NSTC's Subcommittee on Global Change Research. In addition, he/she directs the activities of the National Coordination Office (NCO) in support of the USGCRP. The NCO provides day-to-day coordination and support to the Program. The OSTP and the OMB work closely with the SGCR to establish research priorities and funding plans to ensure that the program is aligned with the national priorities, reflects agency planning, and meets the requirements of the Global Change Research Act, P.L. 101-606.

Interagency Working Groups (IWGs) are the primary USGCRP vehicles for implementing and coordinating research activities within and across agencies. They are critical to Program integration and in assessing progress. New implementation procedures under development will build stronger connections to the SGCR, and increase IWG involvement in developing Program priorities. In creating a revised set of working groups, the Program is emphasizing links to the goals and objectives of the Strategic Plan, coordination across the groups, and better use of the IWGs in framing and implementing Program priorities.

---

22. Sec. 5(c), EO 12881, November 23, 1993.

Tasks within the IWGs will have start and end dates that respond to the IWG accomplishments and evolving Program priorities. The set of working groups will be evaluated periodically through the next decade as interim goals are accomplished.

A number of core USGCRP IWGs align with the Strategic Plan goals and objectives. These groups focus on the following program elements: Integrated Observation, Integrated Modeling, Multidisciplinary Research on the Human and Natural Components of the Earth System, Conduct Sustained Assessments, Informing Decisions, International Cooperation, and Communication and Education. Additional IWGs will be created to address cross-cutting areas of programmatic needs such as information management to provide scientific support in important societal areas. This approach has been piloted successfully over the last two years by the Climate Change and Human Health Group. IWGs will better incorporate biological sciences along with social, behavioral, and economic sciences into the research base of the Program, as discussed in Chapter III. As appropriate, IWG membership will be offered to Federal agencies beyond current USGCRP member agencies to help cultivate new partnerships and incorporate expertise and resources not currently within the Program. USGCRP will also place emphasis on strengthening and developing new relationships with other NSTC subcommittees and working groups, to foster Federal integration beyond USGCRP.

To maximize effectiveness, the Program will employ the best practices from adaptive management— learning and modifying its structure to best respond to the challenges of producing the best science, based on firm data and observations, and explaining impact and options. To do this, USGCRP will work with OSTP, OMB, CEQ, and member agencies as future annual budgets are developed.

Program Planning and Implementation

To realize the USGCRP mission and fully accomplish the Strategic Plan's goals and objectives, the Program is developing a process that links the decadal Strategic Plan to a rolling three-year implementation strategy ("the roadmap"). The roadmap will highlight near- and medium-term Program priorities. This process will enable more effective interagency annual prioritization and longer term budget development. Progress will continue to be reported annually to Congress and the public in *Our Changing Planet*. Drawing from the updated roadmap, the Program will develop the legislatively mandated Revised Research Plan for public comment and publication on a triennial basis.

USGCRP will use these triennial updates, which will incorporate the findings of the ongoing National Assessment regarding gaps and research priorities, as an opportunity to evaluate Program directions, effectiveness, and balance, and to modify plans as necessary to respond to changing conditions and Program progress. USGCRP will continue to consult with the National Research Council to gain a broad, independent, and scientific perspective on the Program direction. The process will also highlight areas where sustained planning and coordination over both the short- and long-term are needed to achieve Program goals, such as observing capability, and data management and service for data-intensive science. Consequently, the process will provide a focus for working group activities.

The intellectual framework provided by the roadmap will be valuable for the USGCRP in developing partnerships. It will help determine which partnerships are most urgently needed and demonstrate the relevance of USGCRP to potential partners. With a three-year time horizon, it will provide a basis for part-ner engagement and participation in USGCRP activities and for discussion of joint new opportunities.

Guidelines for Implementing the Strategic Plan

The following set of guiding principles will assist USGCRP in developing near-, medium-, and long-term priorities over the next 10 years, assessing progress, and developing an effective program portfolio. These guiding principles will help ensure that implementation of the Strategic Plan is both realistic and flexible while maintaining research excellence and increasing the development and application of use-inspired tools and activities. The principles include:

- Ensure continuing strength of the scientific foundation of USGCRP (observations, modeling, and process research), used to support all four Strategic Plan goals

- Develop flexible plans for phasing in activities and priorities over the decade that accommodate budget realities and build upon member agencies' strengths and those of new USGCRP partners

- Develop a portfolio of essential fundamental and new activities that:

  - Maintain consistent and freely available observations

  - Support scientific exploration that best explains underlying processes and impacts on the planet and its populations, and results in having direct societal benefit

  - Emphasize strong collaborations among the USGCRP agencies, facilitated through USGCRP leadership and coordination

  - Enhance transparent access to data and evaluation tools

  - Enable discoveries through transformational research that can lead to breakthroughs in how society understands and responds to global change

  - Build the capacity within USGCRP for interdisciplinary research, especially between the natural science and human components of the Earth system

  - Assist in the translation of science for societal benefit and related risk management decision making

- Build connections within and beyond USGCRP member agencies, and with other interagency bodies that leverage Federal investments and promote the widest use of Program results in supporting the Nation's responses to global change

- Enhance international partnerships that leverage science investments and support assessment and response activities in the United States and globally

- Review progress of interagency activities to evaluate Program priorities

- Use adaptive management principles of evaluation and learning to improve Program outcomes

- Seek input from external groups as appropriate

Annual Prioritization

The Global Change Research Act (Section 105) sets requirements for USGCRP to follow in developing interagency priorities linked to annual budget development. Such shared priorities advance the collective goals of the Program, and also support global change activities in the agencies (and parts of agencies) that fall outside the purview of the current USGCRP program and budgetary portfolios.

Each year, the SGCR develops global change research funding priorities that address science gaps and opportunities, and emerging scientific and societal needs. These shared priorities are intended to provide an advisory framework for the USGCRP agencies to use in setting individual priorities and for communication between the SGCR and OMB regarding Federal priorities in this area, with the goal of promoting interagency cooperation and connectivity to the broad USGCRP directions.

The annual priorities memo will continue to draw from the Strategic Plan, the roadmap, and multi-year priorities from prior years; it may also incorporate any emerging high-priority opportunities. It will highlight priority themes and related activities. A possible theme could emphasize, for example, extremes, potential thresholds, and tipping points in the climate system, and their impacts. For such a theme, integration across the goals could draw on observations, process research and modeling needed to understand extremes in the larger context of changing conditions; the integration of social, behavioral and economic sciences to improve understanding of human responses to rapid change; and the development of national indicators of risk and resilience for assessments that relate to thresholds, tipping points, and extremes.

Prioritization Criteria

In developing both the roadmap and annual priorities, the Program will emphasize the following criteria:

- **Interagency coordination**

  - Involves multiple agencies

  - Focuses on effective ways to achieve priority outcomes

  - Provides opportunities for value-added coordination across two or more agencies (e.g., critical activities in global change research that would be unlikely to get done without USGCRP)

- **Contribution to fundamental understanding**

  - Addresses key theoretical questions, observational needs, process understanding, or modeling uncertainties

  - Extends research to understudied but relevant areas and questions

- **Contribution to improved decision making**

  - Addresses topics that have been identified as decision maker needs or that are key to the Nation's economic vitality, security, or the well-being of its citizens

  - Provides scientific foundations for new solutions or options, especially those that have benefits for other environmental or socioeconomic challenges

  - Contributes useful results that can be communicated effectively to decision makers and affected parties or have the potential to establish ongoing dialogue between researchers and users of scientific information

  - Supports risk assessment and management by improving projections or predictions, providing information on probabilities, clarifying societal consequences of key outcomes, or creating decision-support resources

  - Supports sustained observations at scales needed for science and policy making

- **Feasibility of implementation (practical, institutional, and managerial concerns)**

  - Is ready for implementation (infrastructure, personnel, and facilities are available or could be available to execute the research), or for pilot project status

  - Will provide usable results on timescales relevant for decision making or improved understanding

  - Is cost effective (anticipated outcomes or value of information generated by the activity are sufficient to justify both financial and opportunity costs)

Interagency Collaboration

Collaboration is central to successful implementation of the shared priorities of USGCRP and its member agencies. The collaboration stems from the involvement of multiple agencies in a given area, project or research endeavor that is carried out with full knowledge and appreciation of all the agencies' related and complementary activities. The history of such collaboration is reflected in the Program's annual report to Congress, *Our Changing Planet*. **Box 42** provides an overview of six focus areas for USGCRP for fiscal years 2009–2011, and shows agency participation in the different areas. The pie chart in **Box 43** uses budget information from FY 2010 and shows the percentage of Program investments in the focus areas, relative to the total FY 2010 budget for USGCRP of $2.18 billion. Note that the agencies also carry out a range of activities including observations, and communication and education related to global change, which are not counted as part of the USGCRP budget cross-cut.

Box 42. Focal Areas for Interagency Cooperation, from *Our Changing Planet 2011*

Focus Areas	Participating Agencies
Improving the knowledge of Earth's past and present climate variability and change	DOC*, DOE, DOI, NASA, NSF, SI, USDA
Improving the understanding of natural and human forces of climate change	DOC, DOE, DOI, DOT, EPA, NASA, NSF, USDA
Improving the capability to model and predict future conditions and impacts	DOC, DOE, DOI, HHS, NASA, NSF, SI, USAID, USDA
Assessing the Nation's vulnerability to current and anticipated impacts of climate change	DOC, DOE, DOI, DOT, EPA, NASA, NSF, USDA
Providing climate information and decision support tools	DOC, DOI, DOT, EPA, NASA, NSF, SI, USAID, USDA
Climate change communication and education	DOC, NASA, NSF, SI, USDA

* USGCRP participating organizations from the Department of Commerce (DOC) are the National Institute of Standards and Technology (NIST) and the National Oceanic and Atmospheric Administration (NOAA).

Box 43. FY 2010 U.S. Global Change Research Program Budget by Focus Area[23]

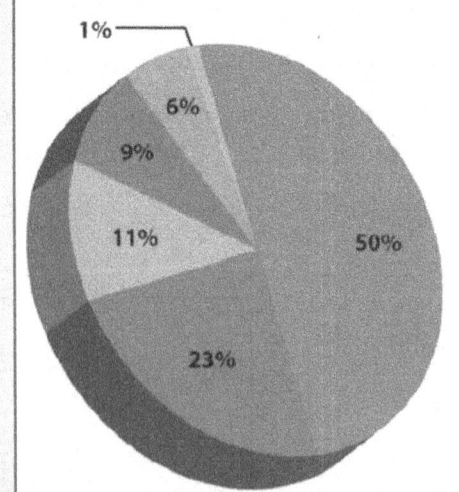

- Improving our knowledge of Earth's past and present climate variability and change
- Improving our understanding of natural and human forces of climate change
- Improving our capability to model and predict future conditions and impacts
- Assessing the Nation's vulnerability to current and anticipated impacts of climate change
- Providing climate information and decision support tools
- Climate change communication and education

Figure: Pie Chart shows shows percentages of the USGCRP budget spent in the indicated focal areas in FY 2010

23. U.S. Global Change Research Program. *Our Changing Planet*, FY11.

To achieve the goals of the Program, USGCRP will need to incorporate the perspectives of those using the research to inform decisions. Answers to questions about who needs the research, what research is needed to inform which decisions, and in what form the research results are needed will be used as inputs to the prioritization process as the USGCRP implements this Strategic Plan.

Partnerships

Partnerships beyond the USGCRP agencies will be important for implementing the full scope of the Strategic Plan over the next decade. One important way to build these partnerships is through the activities related to the Conduct Sustained Assessments goal. The NCA networks extend well beyond the Federal government, and connect with stakeholders in regions and sectors across the country, where the majority of adaptation and mitigation decisions are made. The NCA will be a critical tool for the Program to build capacity and deliver outcomes, particularly as it relates to integration of scientific information that can be used to reduce risk, development of decision support capacity, data management, communications and education, and establishment of research priorities.

The Program will reinforce and expand the strength of current relationships, including those with the CENRS and its subcommittees with natural ties to the USGCRP. It will also incrementally build new partnerships within the Federal government that will help enlist needed expertise (as in the social sciences), incorporate the vantage point of end-use needs into Program direction, and strengthen the Program's support for decision makers.

A key area of expanding partnerships is with other Federal agencies not currently part of USGCRP and with different bureaus in USGCRP agencies that have capabilities needed to help achieve the goals within the Strategic Plan. The Program will work with OSTP and CEQ to systematically identify and begin building relationships, some of which may be with agencies or parts of agencies that have missions outside USGCRP's current focus on research and development. Any such partnerships would be based on complementary strengths and build around current and planned USGCRP activities, such as regional coordination hubs, the Global Change Information System (**Box 23**), and areas of scientific focus such as climate extremes and their impacts and science for use on the scales at which decisions are made. The implementation roadmap will help focus the development of strategic new partnerships and joint activities.

Next Steps

In 2012, the SGCR will evaluate structural and governance aspects of the Program and develop the Implementation Framework for a USGCRP that effectively carries out the Strategic Plan. The Framework will be used to assess and modify, as needed, the mechanisms and operational processes of the USGCRP enterprise, including the SGCR, the NCO, and the IWGs. The Framework will also be developed with the intent of providing appropriate connectivity to NSTC and CENRS, the interagency Climate Change Adaptation Taskforce[24], and other interagency task forces and working groups. Reflective of the adaptive program management approach in the new strategic plan, the Implementation Framework will include periodic internal assessments to ensure that the Program continues to adapt and evolve to always meet the changing needs of society, and provide effective information for enabling decision making by all of the Program's stakeholders.

---

24. For more information, visit http://www.whitehouse.gov/administration/eop/ceq/initiatives/adaptation

Appendix I. Program Activity Description by Agency/Department

The following pages present information about the contributors to USGCRP. For each department, the section titled "Principal Areas of Focus" highlights and summarizes USGCRP-specific activities ongoing within that department or agency.

Department of Agriculture (USDA)

Principal Areas of Focus

The Department of Agriculture's (USDA) global change research program aims to empower land managers, policy makers, and Federal agencies with science-based knowledge to manage the risks, challenges, and opportunities posed by climate change; reduce greenhouse gas emissions; and enhance carbon sequestration. Meeting USDA's goals for expanded economic opportunity, helping rural America thrive, promoting the sustainability of agricultural production, enhancing food security, and conserving natural resources requires understanding climate change's influences and the options for managing them. USDA's global change research program includes contributions from the Agricultural Research Service (ARS), the National Institute of Food and Agriculture (NIFA), the Forest Service, Natural Resources Conservation Service (NRCS), National Agricultural Statistics Service (NASS), and Economic Research Service. USDA draws upon this diversity to identify climate change challenges and priorities in continuing to meet the needs of its stakeholders, decision makers, and collaborators. This work is important to ensuring sustained food security for the Nation and the world; maintaining and enhancing forest and natural resource health; and identifying strategic risks to agricultural production from changing temperature and precipitation as well as pests, disease, and invasive species.

The USDA supports USGCRP on multiple fronts. The Department conducts in-house research and sponsors extramural investigations focused on understanding climate change effects on natural and managed ecosystems, developing the knowledge and tools to enable adaptation under a changing climate, enhancing mitigation of atmospheric greenhouse gases, and providing science-based information for decision support. USDA conducts assessments and projections of climate change impacts on agricultural and natural systems, and develops greenhouse gas inventories. USDA develops cultivars, cropping systems, and management practices to improve drought tolerance and build resilience to climate variability. Conservation systems promoted by the USDA integrate USGCRP research findings into farm and natural resource management, and help build resiliency to climate change on both private and public lands. Development and deployment of decision support tools is a cornerstone of the Department's climate change efforts. USDA maintains critical long-term data collection and observation networks, including the Snowpack Telemetry (SNOTEL) network, the Soil Climate Analysis Network (SCAN), the National Resources Inventory (NRI), and the Forest Inventory and Assessment (FIA). Analysis and modeling work includes biophysical subjects as well as economic analysis of climate change effects and adaptation options. Finally, USDA engages in communication, outreach, and education through multiple forums, including its vast network of agricultural extension services.

Department of Commerce (DOC)

Principal Areas of Focus

The National Oceanic and Atmospheric Administration (NOAA) and the National Institute of Standards and Technology (NIST) comprise the DOC contribution to the USGCRP.

NOAA's strategic climate goal is "an informed society anticipating and responding to climate and its impacts." This is an end-to-end endeavor, and the overall objective is to provide decision makers with a predictive understanding of the climate and to communicate climate information so that people can make more informed decisions in their lives, businesses, and communities. These outcomes are achieved through implementing a global observing system, focused research to understand key climate processes, improved modeling capabilities, and the development and delivery of climate educational programs and information services. NOAA aims to achieve its climate goal through the following strategic objectives:

- Improved scientific understanding of the changing climate system and its impacts

- Assessments of current and future states of the climate system that identify potential impacts and inform science, service, and stewardship decisions

- Mitigation and adaptation efforts supported by sustained, reliable, and timely climate services

- A climate-literate public that understands its vulnerabilities to a changing climate and makes informed decisions

NOAA will advance this goal as it continues to build upon its strong scientific foundation and decades of engagement and collaboration with interagency, academic, international, and private sector partners.

NIST works with other Federal agencies to develop or extend internationally-accepted traceable measurement standards, methodologies, and technologies that enhance measurement capabilities for science-based greenhouse gas emission inventories and measurements critical to advancing climate science research. NIST provides measurements and standards that support accurate, comparable, and reliable climate observations and provides calibrations and special tests to improve the accuracy of a wide range of instruments and techniques used in climate research and monitoring.

Department of Defense (DoD)

Principal Areas of Focus

DoD — while not supporting a formal mission dedicated to global change research — is developing policies and plans to manage and respond to the effects of climate change on DoD missions, assets, and the operational environment. DoD policy calls for a strategic approach to the challenges posed by global climate change and climate variability, which requires an engagement with the Federal research community via the USGCRP. The various research agencies within the DoD often sponsor and undertake basic research activities that concurrently satisfy both national security requirements as well as the strategic goals of the USGCRP. These science and technology investments are coordinated and reviewed by both the Office of the Assistant Secretary of Defense for Research and Engineering and the individual basic research agencies themselves — the Office of Naval Research (ONR), the Air Force Office of Scientific Research (AFOSR), the Army Research Office (ARO), and the Defense Advanced Research Projects Agency (DARPA). When applicable, the research activities of these agencies are coordinated with other federally-sponsored research via the USGCRP and other entities.

In the 2010 Quadrennial Defense Review (QDR), the DoD formally recognized the need to understand and adapt to the impacts of climate change on DoD facilities and military capabilities. The DoD is responsible for the environmental stewardship of hundreds of installations throughout the United States, and must continue incorporating geostrategic and operational energy considerations into force planning, requirements development, and acquisition processes. The DoD relies on the Strategic Environmental Research and Development Program (SERDP), a joint effort among DoD, DOE, and EPA, to develop climate change assessment tools and to identify the environmental variables that must be forecast with sufficient lead time to facilitate appropriate adaptive responses. As the performance of DoD systems and platforms are influenced by environmental conditions, understanding the variability of the Earth's environment and the potential for change is of great interest. Each service agency within the DoD incorporates the potential impact of global change into their long-range strategic plans. For example, the Navy's Task Force Climate Change (TFCC) is the principal Navy organization responsible for advising the Chief of Naval Operations on the impact of climate change on the Navy and assists in the development of science-based recommendations, plans, and actions to adapt to climate change. The U.S. Army Corps of Engineers (USACE) Engineer Research and Development Center (ERDC) Cold Regions Research and Engineering Laboratory (CRREL) also actively investigates the impacts of climate trends for USACE, Army, DoD and other agencies. The CRREL research program responds to the needs of the military, but much of the research also benefits the civilian sector and is funded by non-military customers such as NSF, NOAA, NASA, DOE, and State governments. The DoD regularly reevaluates climate change risks and opportunities in order to develop policies and plans to manage the effects on the Department's operating environment, missions, and facilities.

Department of Energy (DOE)

Principal Areas of Focus

DOE's Office of Science supports fundamental research to understand the energy-environment-climate connection and its implications for energy production, use, sustainability, and security. DOE invests in basic research needed to understand and predict the interactions between critical climate and environmental processes and energy production practices, with particular emphasis on the potential impact of increased anthropogenic emissions. DOE funds research that addresses key uncertainties in the understanding of Earth's complex climate and environmental systems. The scope of the research spans global to submicron scales and includes temporal ranges of processes from nanoseconds to millennia. The research strives for predictive understanding, seeking to provide the foundational science on which to base sound decisions for future energy and environmental challenges. DOE's goal is to advance a robust predictive understanding of Earth's climate and environmental systems and to inform the development of sustainable solutions to the Nation's energy and environmental challenges.

DOE supports three primary research activities along with a national scientific user facility. Two areas of process research focus on identified areas of uncertainty in representing Earth systems in global models: Atmospheric System Research that focuses on the basic science and process studies governing aerosols, clouds, and radiative transfer; and Terrestrial Ecosystem Science that focuses on identifying, under-standing and representing the role of terrestrial ecosystems, and includes support for the AmeriFlux carbon cycle observational network. Through the Climate and Earth System Modeling Program, DOE collaborates with NSF to develop the Community Earth System Model; DOE particularly supports land, atmosphere, aerosols, ocean and cryospheric components, leveraging DOE's leadership high-perfor-mance computing capabilities. DOE modeling supports methods to obtain regional climate information, integrated analysis of climate change impacts, and analysis and distribution of large climate datasets through the Program for Climate Model Diagnosis and Intercomparison and the Earth System Grid. The Atmospheric Radiation Measurement (ARM) Climate Research Facility is a scientific user facility that provides the community with unmatched measurements permitting the most detailed high-resolution, three-dimensional documentation of evolving cloud, aerosol and precipitation characteristics in climate sensitive sites around the world.

To complement basic research carried out by the Office of Science, DOE also conducts applied climate-related research through the CCTP, which is centered in DOE's Office of Policy and International Affairs. CCTP develops and utilizes energy-economic models, including integrated assessment models, to evaluate policies and programs that enable cost-effective greenhouse gas reductions and accelerate the development and deployment of clean energy technologies. As part of this mission CCTP supports work to characterize climate change impacts for use in policy analysis, vulnerability and adaptation assessment and agency rulemakings. DOE also conducts assessments of climate change on electric grid stability, water availability for energy production, and site selection of the next generation of renewable energy infrastructure.

Department of Health and Human Services (HHS)

Principal Areas of Focus

The mission of the U.S. Department of Health and Human Services (HHS) is to enhance the health and well-being of all Americans by providing for effective health and human services and by fostering sound, sustained advances in the sciences underlying medicine, public health, and social services. HHS supports a broad portfolio of research and decision support initiatives related to environmental health and the health effects of global climate change. The National Institutes of Health (NIH) and the Centers for Disease Control and Prevention (CDC) provide the focus for this effort.

Changes in global climate resulting in increases in extremes of heat and precipitation, frequency and intensity of storms, and pervasive changes in water supplies, food systems, and terrestrial and aquatic ecosystems are now having multiple impacts on human health and welfare that are anticipated to continue and increase. These impacts include heat-related morbidity and mortality, respiratory effects of altered air contaminants, changes in transmission of infectious diseases, and impacts in the aftermath of severe weather events. Research is needed to better understand the vulnerabilities of individuals and communities to climate-related changes in health risks. Research is also needed to assess the effective-ness of various public health adaptation strategies to reduce climate vulnerability, as well as the potential health effects of interventions to reduce greenhouse gas emissions.

HHS supports all four goal areas of the Global Change Research Program: Advance Science, Inform Decisions, Conduct Sustained Assessments, and Communicate and Educate. By conducting fundamental and applied research on the linkages between climate change and health, translating scientific advances into decision support tools for public health professionals, conducting ongoing monitoring and surveillance of climate-related health outcomes, and disseminating scientific information and engaging the public health community in two-way communication, HHS provides a model of the "end to end" science paradigm the GCRP seeks to achieve.

The NIH's National Institute of Environmental Health Sciences (NIEHS) and CDC co-chair (along with NOAA) the USGCRP's Climate Change and Human Health Interagency Working Group of the USGCRP. In addition, both NIEHS and CDC serve on the health technical input team to the National Climate Assessment, which seeks to provide the scientific information that can be used by communities around the country to effectively plan for adaptation and mitigation.

The CDC's Climate and Health Program leads efforts to prevent and adapt to the anticipated health impacts associated with the changing climate. Through interdisciplinary work with local and state health departments, research institutions, and other Federal agencies, the CDC identifies populations most vulnerable to climate impacts, anticipates future trends, assures that systems are in place to detect and respond to emerging health threats, and takes steps to assure that these health risks can be managed now and in the future.

The NIEHS and Fogarty International Center lead NIH efforts to develop a robust research program on the human health impacts of climate change. The results of this program will help to inform climate change adaptation and guide public health interventions to reduce harm to the most vulnerable communities. The NIH also supports a large research portfolio relevant to the human health impacts of climate change, including but not limited to the direct health impacts of increased temperatures and extreme weather events, the health effects of air pollution and aeroallergens, water quality and quantity, ecosystem influences on infectious disease transmission, and potential health effects of materials used in new technologies to mitigate or adapt to climate change.

Department of the Interior (DOI)

Principal Areas of Focus

The Department of Interior (DOI) is both a natural resource management agency and a science agency. The U.S. Geological Survey (USGS) conducts global change research for DOI and comprises DOI's contribution to USGCRP. Several other DOI bureaus also contribute to the goals of the USGCRP Strategic Plan through activities such as monitoring, science translation to inform decisions, impact assessments, adaptation planning, and communication and education.

USGS scientists have worked in collaboration with other USGCRP agencies to meet the pressing needs of policy makers and resource managers for scientifically valid state-of-the-science information and predictive understanding of global change and its effects. The USGS Climate and Land Use Change mission leads research, adaptation, and mitigation activities to help the Nation understand, adapt to, and mitigate global change and its impacts on society, resource availability, and economic development.

USGS studies contribute directly to the strategic goals and core competencies of the USGCRP. The USGS Climate and Land Use Change Research and Development Program supports research to understand processes controlling Earth system responses to global change and model impacts of climate and land-cover change on natural resources in a range of environments, from the Arctic to the tropics. USGS geographic analyses and land remote-sensing programs (such as the Landsat satellite mission and the National Land Cover Database) provide data that can be used to assess changes in land use and land cover, ecosystems, and water resources resulting from the interactions between human activities and natural systems. The science products and data sets from these programs are essential for conducting quantitative studies of carbon storage and greenhouse gas flux in the Nation's ecosystems. Over the past three years, the USGS has developed scientifically based methods for assessment of biologic and geologic carbon sequestration, and the USGS is currently completing the assessments called for in the Energy Independence and Security Act of 2007.

The USGS National Climate Change and Wildlife Science Center is leading the establishment of eight DOI regional Climate Science Centers that will address the research and management needs of partners by providing science and technical support regarding the impacts of climate change on fish, wildlife, and ecological processes. The DOI Climate Science Centers will provide robust predictive and empirical tools for natural resource managers to test adaptive strategies, reduce risk, and increase the potential for hydrologic and ecological systems to be self-sustaining, resilient, or adaptable to climate change and other disturbances.

Department of State (DOS)

Principal Areas of Focus

Through Department of State (DOS) annual funding, the United States is the world's leading financial contributor to the United Nations Framework Convention on Climate Change (UNFCCC) and to the Intergovernmental Panel on Climate Change (IPCC)—the principal international organization for the assessment of scientific, technical, and socioeconomic information relevant to the understanding of climate change, its potential impacts, and options for adaptation and mitigation. Recent DOS contributions to these organizations provide substantial support for global climate observation and assessment activities in developing countries. DOS also works with other agencies in promoting international cooperation in a range of bilateral and multilateral climate change initiatives and partnerships.

Department of Transportation (DOT)

Principal Areas of Focus

The Department of Transportation (DOT) conducts research and uses existing science to improve climate change decision making. DOT research examines the potential climate change impacts on transportation, and methods of increasing transportation efficiency and reducing emissions. Many DOT programs have either direct or indirect climate benefits and support USGCRP areas of focus.

The Department's focal point for information and technical expertise on climate change is the Center for Climate Change. The Center coordinates transportation and climate change research, policies, and actions within DOT. The Center promotes comprehensive approaches to reduce emissions, prepares for climate change impacts, develops adaptation strategies and conducts outreach activities.

DOT participates in the work of the National Climate Assessment both directly and through focused research such as the Center's Gulf Coast Studies. DOT is identifying strategies to integrate adaptation planning into transportation policies, programs and operations.

The Federal Highway Administration, the Federal Transit Administration and other DOT agencies are undertaking: climate impact and adaptation studies (including vulnerability and risk assessments); work with science agencies to develop regional climate data and projections; methodological research; supporting pilot programs; and providing assistance to transportation stakeholders including State and local agencies.

The Federal Aviation Administration (FAA) works to identify and assess potential measures to reduce fuel consumption and greenhouse gas emissions. FAA conducts research to support USGCRP by: working with NASA, NOAA, and EPA in the Aviation Climate Change Research Initiative (ACCRI), to identify and address key scientific gaps and uncertainties regarding aviation climate impacts and inform mitigation; working with NASA and Transport Canada in the Partnership for Air Transportation Noise and Emissions Reduction (PARTNER) Center of Excellence, which fosters advances in alternative fuels, emissions, noise, operations, and aircraft technologies; conducting research to support ongoing operational initiatives to reduce fuel consumption and aviation emissions, including improved air traffic management, and the Voluntary Airport Low-Emissions program that helps deploy low-emissions technologies to airports; and participating in the International Civil Aviation Organization's Committee on Aviation Environmental Protection, and provides technical expertise and data to the IPCC and the UNFCCC.

Other DOT initiatives that address climate change and improve the sustainability of the U.S. transportation sector include: The FAA and NASA manage the Continuous Lower Energy, Emissions, and Noise (CLEEN) program as a government industry consortium to develop technologies for energy efficiency, noise and emissions reduction, and alternative fuels; FAA participates in the Commercial Aviation Alternative Fuels Initiative (CAAFI), a public-private coalition to encourage the development of alternative jet fuels; and the National Highway Traffic Safety Administration (NHTSA) conducts research in support of joint DOT/EPA rulemakings to improve the fuel economy of on-road vehicles.

Environmental Protection Agency (EPA)

Principal Areas of Focus

The core purpose of EPA's Global Change Research Program is to develop scientific information that supports stakeholders, policymakers, and society at large as they respond to climate change and associated impacts on human health, ecosystems, and socioeconomic systems in the United States. EPA's research is focused on topics driven by the Agency's mission and statutory requirements, and includes: (1) improving the scientific understanding of global change effects on air quality, water quality, ecosystems, and human health in the context of other stressors; (2) assessing and developing adaptation options to effectively respond to global change risks, increase resilience of human and natural systems, and promote their sustainability; and (3) developing an understanding of the potential environmental impacts and benefits of greenhouse gas emission reduction strategies to support sustainable mitigation solutions. EPA's program emphasizes the integration of knowledge across the physical, chemical, biological, and social sciences into decision support frameworks that recognize the complex interactions between human and natural systems at national, regional and local scales. This information is further leveraged by EPA Program Offices and Regions in support of mitigation and adaptation analyses, decisions, and efforts, and to promote communication with external stakeholders and the public.

EPA relies on the Program to develop high-quality scientific data and understanding about physical, chemical, and biological changes to the global environment and their relation to drivers of global change. EPA's Global Change Research Program connects these results to specific human and ecosystem health endpoints in ways that enable local, regional, and national decision makers to develop and implement strategies to protect human health and the environment. In turn, EPA's research provides USGCRP agencies with information about the connections between global change and local impacts and how local actions influence global changes.

Research activities include efforts to connect continental-scale temperature and precipitation changes to regional and local air quality and hydrology models to better understand the impacts of climate change on air quality and water quality, and to examine how watersheds will respond to large-scale climate and other global changes to inform decisions about management of aquatic ecosystems and expand understanding of the impacts of global change. Satellite and other observational efforts conducted by USGCRP are crucial to supporting EPA's efforts to understand how land use change, climate change, and other global changes are affecting watersheds and ecosystems, and the services they provide.

National Aeronautics and Space Administration (NASA)

Principal Areas of Focus

The 2010 National Space Policy stated that NASA plays a crucial role in global change research and sustained monitoring capabilities, and advances scientific knowledge of the global integrated Earth system through satellite observations and development of new Earth observing satellites. In accomplishing this mandate, NASA's comprehensive and integrated program on satellite instrument development, observations and modeling, science and technology research, and education and applications will fully support the new USGCRP Strategic Plan to advance science, inform decisions, sustain assessments, and communicate and educate. NASA's funding contribution to the USGCRP equals the total amount of all other USGCRP agency contributions.

NASA's global change activities have four integrated foci: satellite observations; technology development; research and analysis; and applications. Satellites provide critical global atmosphere, ocean, land, sea ice, and ecosystem measurements with frequent sampling in time and space with uniform accuracy and stability. NASA's sixteen on-orbit satellites measure numerous variables required to enhance understanding of Earth interactions. The oldest on-orbit satellite was launched in 1997; it and eleven others have exceeded their prime mission lifetimes and provide data through mission extensions. In 2011, NASA launched two satellites (June – sea surface salinity [Aquarius/SAC[25]-D]; October – atmospheric and oceanic data continuity [NPP[26]]). In 2013, NASA intends to launch the Landsat Data Continuity Mission (LDCM) satellite to measure land cover and evapotranspiration. Other satellites are in development for launch in 2014 and beyond.

Technology development enables advanced space-based instruments and information technologies. Science research and analysis of satellite observations and model results inform development of satellite missions and improve predictability and knowledge of the global integrated Earth system. Piloted and unattended airborne systems enable calibration/validation of satellite data, provide measurements

---

25. Satelite de Aplicaiones Científicas
26. National Polar-orbiting Operational Environmental Satellite System (NPOESS) Preparatory Project

with horizontal and vertical resolutions beyond the capabilities of satellites, and test prototype instruments. Themes of five major airborne campaigns scheduled for FY 2012 are: north and south polar seas and ice sheets; atmospheric composition and clouds over southeast Asia; carbon storage and flux in the Arctic; hurricanes in the Atlantic Ocean; and root-zone soil moisture at different locales in North America. An oceanic campaign to observe salinity processes in the North Atlantic Ocean is scheduled for FY 2012. NASA promotes new intellectual capacity through educational opportunities and provides opportunities for new applications of satellite observations to public and private organizations. NASA actively contributes toward interdisciplinary assessments such as the National Climate Assessment and international global climate, marine, and ozone assessments. About one thousand researchers are funded through an open, transparent peer-review proposal process.

National Science Foundation (NSF)

Principal Areas of Focus

The National Science Foundation (NSF) programs address global change issues through investments that advance frontiers of knowledge, provide state-of-the-art instrumentation and facilities, develop new analytical methods, and enable cross-disciplinary collaborations while also cultivating a diverse highly trained workforce and developing resources for public education. In particular, NSF global change programs support the research and related activities to advance fundamental understanding of physical, chemical, biological, and human systems and the interactions among them. The programs encourage interdisciplinary approaches to studying Earth system processes and the consequences of change, including how humans respond to changing environments and the impacts on ecosystems and the essential services they provide. NSF programs promote the enhancement of models to improve understanding of integrated Earth system processes and to advance predictive capability. NSF also supports fundamental research on the processes used by organizations and decision makers to identify and evaluate policies for mitigation, adaptation, and other responses to the challenge of a changing and variable environment. Long-term, continuous and consistent observational records are essential for testing hypotheses quantitatively and are thus a cornerstone of global change research. NSF supports a variety of research observing networks that complement, and are dependent on, the climate monitoring systems maintained by its sister agencies. NSF regularly collaborates with other USGCRP agencies to provide support for a range of multi-disciplinary research projects and is actively engaged in a number of international partnerships.

Smithsonian Institution (SI)

Principal Areas of Focus

Within the Smithsonian Institution, global change research is primarily conducted at the National Air and Space Museum, the National Museum of Natural History, the National Zoological Park, the Smithsonian Astrophysical Observatory, the Smithsonian Environmental Research Center, and the Smithsonian Tropical Research Institute. The unique research contribution of the Smithsonian Institution is a long-term perspective—for example, undertaking investigations that may require extended study before producing useful results and conducting observations on sufficiently long (e.g., decadal) timescales to resolve human-caused modification of natural variability. Research is organized around themes of atmospheric processes, ecosystem dynamics, observing natural and anthropogenic environmental change on multiple timescales, and defining longer term climate proxies present in the historical artifacts and records of the museums as well as in the geologic record. Most of these units participate in the Smithsonian Institution Group on Earth Observations (SIGEO) examining the dynamics of forests over decadal time frames. The Smithsonian Grand Challenge Consortium for Understanding and Sustaining a Biodiverse Planet brings together researchers from around the Institution to focus on joint programs ranging from estimating volcanic emissions to ocean acidification measurement. Smithsonian paleontological research documents and interprets the history of terrestrial and marine ecosystems from 400 million years ago to the present. Other scientists study the impacts of historical environmental change on the ecology and evolution of organisms, including humans. Archaeobiologists examine the impact of early humans resulting from their domestication of plants and animals, creating the initial human impacts on planetary ecosystems. USGCRP funding enables the Smithsonian to leverage private funds for additional research and education programs. Scientific data from different research programs are made available through internet access and upon request to users around the world. The Smithsonian is increasing its digitization of historic data that are not currently available in digital form (e.g., only stored in paper files or specimen labels), or are not currently available in formats that support community access. Units previously mentioned are joined by our history and art units, such as the Center for Folklife and Cultural History, the National Museum of the American Indian, and the Cooper Hewitt Museum of Design to examine human responses to global change, within communities, reflected in art and culture, food and music. Smithsonian outreach and education expands our scientific and social understanding of processes of change and represent them in exhibits and programs, including at the history and art museums of the Smithsonian.

U.S. Agency for International Development (USAID)

Principal Areas of Focus

The U.S. Agency for International Development (USAID) supports a number of programs that enable decision makers to apply high-quality climate information to decision making. USAID's climate change and development strategy calls for enabling countries to accelerate their transition to climate resilient, low emission sustainable economic development through direct programming and integrating climate change adaptation and mitigation objectives across the Agency's development portfolio. USAID is the lead contributor to bilateral assistance, with a focus on capacity building, civil society building, and governance programming, and creating the legal and regulatory environments needed to address climate change. USAID leverages scientific and technical resources from across the government (e.g., NASA, NOAA, USDA, USGS) as it applies its significant technical expertise to provide leadership in development and implementation of low-emissions development strategies, creating policy frameworks for market-based approaches to emission reduction and energy sector reform, promoting sustainable management of agriculture lands and forests, and mainstreaming adaptation into development activities in countries most at risk. USAID has long-standing relationships with host country governments that enable it to work together to develop shared priorities and implementation plans. USAID's engagement and expertise in agriculture, biodiversity, infrastructure, and other critical climate sensitive sectors provide an opportunity to implement innovative cross-sectoral climate change programs. Finally, USAID bilateral programs work in key political and governance areas multilateral agencies cannot.

Appendix II. Glossary of Terms

Abrupt climate change: Rapid climate change occurring at timescales faster than the typical timescale of the responsible forcing. Possible abrupt events that have been proposed include rapid deglaciation and massive melting of permafrost or increases in soil respiration leading to fast changes in the carbon cycle.[27]

Adaptation: Adjustment in natural and/or human systems to a new or changing environment that exploits beneficial opportunities and moderates negative impacts.

Adaptive capacity (in relation to climate and global change impacts): The ability of a system to adjust to climate and global change (including climate variability and extremes) to moderate potential damages, to take advantage of opportunities, or to cope with the consequences.[28]

Adaptive management: Process that focuses on learning and adapting through partnerships of managers, scientists, and stakeholders who learn together how to improve outcomes. Operational decisions, principally for managing entities that are influenced by climate variability and change. These decisions can apply to the management of infrastructure (e.g., a wastewater treatment plant), the integrated management of a natural resource (e.g., a watershed), or the operation of societal response mechanisms (e.g., health alerts, water restrictions). Adaptive management operates within existing policy frameworks or uses existing infrastructure, and the decisions usually occur on timescales of a year or less.

Aerosols: Fine solid or liquid particles suspended in a gas. Aerosols may be of either natural or anthropogenic origin.[29] The climatic effects of aerosols are important but incompletely understood. Aerosols can have non-climatic environmental and health impacts.

Albedo: The fraction of solar radiation reflected by a surface or object, often expressed as a percentage.[30]

Anthropogenic: Resulting from or produced by human beings.

Arctic Climate Impact Assessment (2004): An international project, of the Arctic Council and the International Arctic Science Committee, to evaluate and synthesize knowledge on climate variability, climate change, and increased ultraviolet radiation and their consequences in the Arctic region.

Argo float array: Argo is a global array of 3,000 free-drifting profiling floats that measures the temperature and salinity of the upper 2000 m of the ocean. This allows for continuous monitoring of the temperature, salinity, and velocity of the upper ocean.

---

27. IPCC Fourth Assessment Report. Climate Change 2007: The Physical Science Basis. Contribution of Working Group I to the Fourth Assessment Report of the Intergovernmental Panel on Climate Change, 2007. Solomon, S.,D. Qin, M. Manning, Z. Chen, M. Marquis, K.B. Averyt, M. Tignor and H.L. Miller (eds.) Cambridge University Press, Cambridge, United Kingdom and New York, NY.

28. *Ibid.*

29. John H. Seinfeld, Spyros N. Pandis. 2006. Atmospheric Chemistry and Physics: From Air Pollution to Climate Change. 2nd ed. John Wiley & Sons, Inc. Hoboken, New Jersey.

30. IPCC, 2007.

Assessments: Processes that involve analyzing and evaluating the state of scientific knowledge (and the associated degree of scientific certainty) and, in interaction with users, stakeholders, etc., developing information applicable to a particular set of issues or decisions.

Atmosphere: The gaseous envelope surrounding Earth.[31]

Belmont Forum: A collaborative mechanism among international organizations, such as the International Council for Science (ICSU), and national funding agencies to identify global change research priorities that might benefit from better cooperation and to determine how to best address them.

Biodiversity: The total diversity of all organisms and ecosystems at various spatial scales.[32]

Biofuel: Any liquid, gaseous, or solid fuel produced from plant or animal organic matter, for example, soybean oil, alcohol from fermented sugar, and wood. This term includes items such as ethanol and biodiesel derived from biomass by chemical or biological processes (also known as second-generation biofuels).

Biomass: The total mass of living organisms in a given area or volume.[33]

Biosphere: The part of the Earth system comprising all ecosystems and living organisms, in the atmosphere, on land or in the ocean, including derived dead organic matter, such as litter, soil organic matter, and oceanic detritus.[34]

Biogeochemical cycle: A pathway by which a chemical element, such as carbon, nitrogen or phosphorus, or a compound, like water, moves through Earth's biosphere, atmosphere, hydrosphere, and/or lithosphere.

Black carbon: Also known as "soot." Black carbon is produced both naturally and by human activities as a result of the incomplete combustion of fossil fuels, biofuels, and biomass. Black carbon particles strongly absorb sunlight and give soot its black color. They have important health impacts as well.

Carbon cycle: The term used to describe the flow of carbon (in various forms, e.g., as carbon dioxide, calcium carbonate) through the atmosphere, ocean, terrestrial biosphere, and/or lithosphere.[35]

Carbon, nitrogen, and phosphorus cycling: See *biogeochemical cycle.*

Carbon sequestration: The process of increasing the carbon content of a carbon reservoir other than the atmosphere. Can be performed deliberately as a way of slowing the buildup of CO_2 in the atmosphere.

Climate: The mean and variability of relevant measures of the atmosphere-ocean system over periods ranging from weeks to thousands or millions of years.[36]

---

31. Seinfeld and Pandis, 2006
32. IPCC, 2007.
33. *Ibid.*
34. *Ibid.*
35. *Ibid.*
36. *Ibid.*

Climate change: A statistically significant variation in either the mean state of the climate or in its variability, persisting for an extended period (typically decades or longer). Climate change may be due to natural internal processes or to external forcing, including changes in solar radiation and volcanic eruptions, or to persistent human-induced changes in atmospheric composition or in land use. See also *climate variability.*[37]

Climate feedback: See *feedback.*

Climate model: A numerical representation of the climate system based on the mathematical equations governing the physical, chemical, and biological properties of its components and including treatment of key physical processes and interactions, cast in a form suitable for numerical approximation making use of computers.[38]

Climate prediction: A climate prediction or climate forecast is the result of an attempt to produce an estimate of the actual evolution of the climate in the future, for example, at seasonal, interannual, or long-term timescales.[39]

Climate projection: A projection of the response of the climate system to emission or concentration scenarios of greenhouse gases and aerosols, or radiative forcing scenarios, often based upon simulations by climate models. Climate projections are distinguished from climate predictions in order to emphasize that climate projections depend upon the emission/concentration/radiative forcing scenario used, which are based on assumptions concerning, for example, future socioeconomic and technological developments that may or may not be realized and are therefore subject to substantial uncertainty.[40]

Climate system: The highly complex system consisting of five major components: the atmosphere, the hydrosphere, the cryosphere, the land surface, and the biosphere, and the interactions among them.[41]

Climate variability: Variations in the mean state and other statistics (such as the occurrence of extremes, etc.) of the climate on all temporal and spatial scales beyond that of individual weather events. These variations are often due to internal processes within the climate system (internal variability), or to variations in natural or anthropogenic external forcing (external variability).[42]

Committee on Environment, Natural Resources, and Sustainability (CENRS): A subcommittee of the National Science and Technology Council (NSTC) established to assist the NSTC in increasing the overall productivity and application of Federal research and development efforts in the areas of environment, natural resources, and sustainability, and to provide a formal mechanism for interagency coordination in these areas. CENRS encompasses the Subcommittee on Global Change Research, the steering committee of the United States Global Change Research Program.

Community Earth System Model: A specific global climate model developed by USGCRP agencies and academic collaborators that is used to simulate the many components of Earth's climate system, including the ocean, atmosphere, sea ice, and land cover.

---

37. *IPCC, 2007.*
38. IPCC, 2007, and National Snow and Ice Data Center.
39. IPCC, 2007.
40. *Ibid.*
41. *Ibid.*
42. *Ibid.*

Complex system: A system composed of interconnected parts that as a whole exhibit one or more properties not obvious from the properties of individual parts.

Cryosphere: The region of the Earth that is perennially frozen, including all snow, ice, and frozen ground (including permafrost) on and beneath the surface of the Earth and ocean.

Data assimilation: The often iterative process of combining a model with observational data to provide an estimate of the state of a system. Data assimilation is typically used to develop information for places and times where no observations were made.

Decision support: The provision of timely and useful information that addresses specific questions.

Downscaling: A method that derives local- to regional-scale (10 to 100 km) information from larger-scale (100 to 1000 km) models or data analyses.[43]

Earth system: The unified set of physical, chemical, biological, and social components, processes and interactions that together determine the state and dynamics of planet Earth.

Earth System Modeling Framework: Open-source software for building and coupling weather, climate, and related models.

Ecosystem: A system of living organisms interacting with each other and their physical environment as an ecological unit.

Ecosystem services: The conditions and processes through which natural ecosystems, and the species that make them up, sustain and fulfill human life. Examples include provision of clean water, maintenance of livable climates, pollination of crops and native vegetation, and fulfillment of people's cultural, spiritual, intellectual needs.[44]

El Niño Southern Oscillation (ENSO): An important form of natural climate variability occurring on a timescale of 2 to 7 years. ENSO is characterized by variations in sea surface temperatures in the tropical Pacific Ocean, accompanied by variations in atmospheric surface pressure in specific locations. The opposite phases of ENSO are known as El Niño and La Niña, and are associated with widespread variations in temperature and precipitation patterns.

Emergent behavior: The feature of complex systems by which cause-effect relationships between individual components at the subsystem level are not additive or aggregate in simple ways when all of the components are linked to form the system. Emergent properties of the system as a whole appear.[45]

Emissions: In the climate change context, emissions refer to the release of radiatively or chemically active substances (e.g., greenhouse gases and/or their precursors, aerosols) into the atmosphere over a specified area and period of time.

---

43. IPCC, 2007
44. Daily, G. Ed. (1997). Nature's Services (Island Press, Washington, DC, 1997); Conserv. Ecol. http://www.consecol. org/vol3/iss2/art14 (1999).
45. "Steffen et al., 2004. Global Change and the Earth System: A Planet Under Pressure. International Geosphere-Biosphere Programme (IGBP).

Executive Order 13514 (Federal Leadership in Environmental, Energy, and Economic Performance): A 2009 Executive Order to establish an integrated strategy towards sustainability in the Federal government and to make reduction of greenhouse gas emissions a priority for Federal agencies.

Exposure: In the context of vulnerability to climate change, exposure refers to the climate-related stressors that influence particular systems, and can include stressors such as droughts (e.g., in the context of water resources, agriculture, forestry) or sea-level rise (e.g., coastal flooding, habitat loss).[46]

Extreme weather event: An event that is rare at a particular place and time of year. Definitions of "rare" vary, but an extreme weather event would normally be as rare as or rarer than the 10th or 90th percentile of the observed probability density of weather events.[47]

Feedback: An interaction mechanism between processes such that the result of an initial process triggers changes in a second process and that in turn influences the initial one. A positive feedback intensifies the original process, and a negative feedback reduces it.[48]

General Circulation (GCM) or Atmosphere/Ocean Global Climate Model: A numerical representation of the climate system based on the physical and chemical properties of its components, their interactions and feedback processes, and accounting for all or some of its known properties.[49]

Geoengineering: Deliberate large-scale manipulation of the planetary environment as a strategy to counteract anthropogenic climate change.[50]

Global change: Changes in the global environment (including alterations in climate, land productivity, oceans or other water resources, atmospheric composition and/or chemistry, and ecological systems) that may alter the capacity of the Earth to sustain life.[51]

Global Change Information System: An information system under development through the USGCRP that establishes data interfaces and interoperable repositories of climate and global change data which can be easily and efficiently accessed, integrated with other data sets, maintained over time and expanded as needed into the future.

Global change research: Study, monitoring, assessment, prediction, and information management activities to describe and understand the interactive physical, chemical, and biological processes that regulate the total Earth system; the unique environment that the Earth provides for life; changes that are occurring in the Earth system; and the manner in which such system, environment, and changes are influenced by human actions.

Global Change Research Act of 1990: An act establishing the United States Global Change Research Program, an interagency program aimed at understanding and responding to global change, including the cumulative effects of human activities and natural processes on the environment, to promote discussions toward international protocols in global change research, and for other purposes.

---

46. Daily, G. Ed. (1997). *Nature's Services* (Island Press, Washington, DC, 1997); Conserv. Ecol. http://www.consecol.org/vol3/iss2/art14 (1999).
47. IPCC, 2007.
48. *Ibid*.
49. *Ibid*.
50. National Research Council's America's Climate Choices: Advancing the Science of Climate Change, 2010.
51. Global Change Research Act of 1990.

Global Earth Observing System of Systems (GEOSS): A "system of systems" linking together existing and planned observing systems around the world and promoting common technical standards so that data from thousands of different instruments can be combined into coherent data sets.

Global Framework for Climate Services (GFCS): An outcome of the World Climate Conference (WCC-3) of the United Nations World Meteorological Organization, with the goal of the development and provision of relevant science-based climate information and prediction for climate risk management and adaptation to climate variability and change, throughout the world.

Greenhouse effect: Trapping and build-up of infrared radiation (heat) in the atmosphere (troposphere) near the Earth's surface. Some of the heat flowing back toward space from Earth's surface is absorbed by water vapor, carbon dioxide, ozone, and several other gases in the atmosphere and then reradiated back toward Earth's surface. If the atmospheric concentrations of these greenhouse gases rise, the average temperature of the lower atmosphere will gradually increase.[52]

Greenhouse gas: Any gas that absorbs infrared radiation (heat) in the atmosphere. Greenhouse gases include, but are not limited to, water vapor, carbon dioxide, methane, nitrous oxide, chlorofluorocarbons, hydro chlorofluorocarbons, ozone, hydro fluorocarbons, perfluorocarbons, and sulfur hexafluoride.[53]

Human system: Any system in which human organizations play a major role. Often, but not always, the term is synonymous with "society" or "social system," for example, agricultural system, political system, technological system, or economic system.[54]

Human-natural system: Integrated systems in which human and natural components interact, such as the interaction between socioeconomic and biophysical processes in urban ecosystems.[55]

Hydrologic cycle: The flow of water through the Earth system via the processes of evaporation, vertical and horizontal transport of vapor, condensation, precipitation, and the flow of water from continents to the ocean.

Hydrologic systems: The systems involved in movement, distribution, and quality of water throughout Earth, including both the hydrologic cycle and water resources.[56]

Impacts, Adaptation, Vulnerability (IAV) models: Models of specific socioeconomic sectors or systems of particular societal interest, such as agriculture, coasts, energy, transportation, health, forestry, fisheries, and water resources, that can be used to investigate the sensitivity of these sectors and systems to climate and global change to support both process understanding and decision making.

In situ: Measurements obtained through instruments that are in direct contact with the subject (e.g., a soil thermometer), as opposed to those collected by remote instruments (e.g., a radar altimeter).

Integrated Assessment Models (IAMs): A method of analysis that combines results and models from the physical, biological, economic, and social sciences, and the interactions between these components, in a consistent framework to evaluate the status and consequences of environmental change and the policy responses to it.

---

52. EPA, Glossary of Climate Change Terms, http://www.epa.gov/climatechange/glossary.html
53. *Ibid.*
54. IPCC, 2007.
55. Urban Ecology Research Laboratory, University of Washington.
56. IPCC, 2007.

Intergovernmental Panel on Climate Change (IPCC): An international scientific body for the assessment of climate change, established by the United Nations Environment Programme and the United Nations World Meteorological Organization.

Land cover: The physical material covering the surface of the earth including vegetation (forests, shrub lands, crops, deserts, lawns), bare soil, developed surfaces (paved land, buildings), and bodies of water (watercourses, wetlands).

Land use: The total of arrangements, activities and inputs undertaken in a certain land cover type (a set of human actions). The term land use is also used in the sense of the social and economic purposes for which land is managed (e.g., grazing, timber extraction and conservation).[57]

Land use and land cover change: A change in the use or management of land by humans that may lead to a change in land cover.[58]

Metadata: Information about meteorological and climatological data concerning how and when they were measured, their quality, known problems, and other characteristics.[59]

Mitigation (climate change): An intervention to reduce the sources or enhance the sinks of greenhouse gases and other climate warming agents. This intervention could include approaches devised to reduce emissions of greenhouse gases to the atmosphere; to enhance their removal from the atmosphere through storage in geological formations, soils, biomass, or the ocean.

Monitoring: A scientifically designed system of continuing standardized measurements and observations and their evaluation. Monitoring is specifically intended to continue over long time periods.

Montreal Protocol on Substances that Deplete the Ozone Layer (1987): An international treaty designed to reduce the production and consumption of ozone depleting substances in order to reduce their abundance in the atmosphere, and thereby protect the Earth's fragile ozone layer.[60]

Nonlinearity: A process in which there is no simple proportional relation between cause and effect.[61]

National Climate Assessment (NCA): An assessment conducted under the auspices of the Global Change Research Act of 1990, which requires a report to the President and the Congress every four years that evaluates, integrates and interprets the findings of the United States Global Change Research Program with the intent to advance an inclusive and sustained process for assessing and communicating scientific knowledge of the impacts, risks and vulnerabilities associated with a changing global climate in support of decision making across the United States.

National Research Council: An arm of the National Academy of Sciences that forms committees to enlist the Nation's top scientists, engineers, and other experts to provide independent advice to the government on matters of science, technology, and medicine.

---

57. IPCC, 2007.
58. *Ibid.*
59. *Ibid.*
60. From United Nations Environment Programme.
61. IPCC, 2007

National Science and Technology Council (NSTC): A Cabinet-level Council established by Executive Order that is the principal means within the executive branch to coordinate science and technology policy across the diverse entities that make up the Federal research and development enterprise.

Observations: Measurements (either continuing or episodic) of variables in climate and related systems.

Observing system: A coordinated series of instruments for long-term observations of the land surface, biosphere, solid Earth, atmosphere, and/or oceans to improve understanding of Earth as an integrated system.

Ocean acidification: The phenomenon in which the pH of the ocean becomes more acidic due to increased levels of carbon dioxide in the atmosphere from human activities, which, in turn, increase the amount of dissolved carbon dioxide in seawater. Ocean acidification may lead to reduced calcification rates of calcifying organisms such as corals, mollusks, algae and crustacea.

Office of Science and Technology Policy (OSTP): A division of the Executive Office of the President (EOP) established by Congress in 1976 with a broad mandate to advise the President and others within the EOP on the effects of science and technology on domestic and international affairs. The 1976 Act also authorizes OSTP to lead interagency efforts to develop and implement sound science and technology policies and budgets, and to work with the private sector, state and local governments, the science and higher education communities, and other nations toward this end.

Ozone: A colorless gas consisting of three atoms of oxygen, readily reacting with many other substances. Ground-level or surface ozone (tropospheric ozone) contributes to smog and poor air quality and is harmful to human health. Ozone higher up in the atmosphere ("stratospheric ozone") plays a dominant role in the stratospheric radiative balance and shields the ground from harmful UV radiation. Ozone also acts as a greenhouse gas.

Ozone hole: A severe depletion of the ozone layer in the Earth's atmosphere over the Antarctic region caused by anthropogenic chlorine and bromine compounds in combination with the specific meteorological conditions of that region. See *scientific assessments of ozone depletion*. Ozone depletion occurs beyond the Antarctic as well.

Paleoclimate: Climate on the scale of the entire history of Earth and before human-recorded climate data using instrumentation. Paleodata are preserved within natural resources such as corals, rocks, ocean and lake sediments, ice cores, tree rings, shells, and microfossils and extend the archive of weather and climate back hundreds to millions of years.

Parameterization: In climate models, this term refers to the technique of representing processes that cannot be explicitly resolved at the space or time resolution of the model (subgrid-scale processes) by relationships between model-resolved larger-scale flow and the area- or time-averaged effect of such subgrid-scale processes.[62]

Permafrost: Ground (soil or rock and including water, ice, and organic material) that remains at or below freezing for at least two consecutive years.[63]

---

62. IPCC, 2007
63. *Ibid.*

Radiative forcing: A process that acts to changes the average energy balance of the Earth-atmosphere system by affecting the balance between incoming solar radiation and outgoing radiation. A positive forcing warms the surface of the Earth and a negative forcing cools the surface.

Remote sensing: The technique of obtaining information about objects through the analysis of data collected by instruments that are not in physical contact with the object of investigation. In a climate context, remote sensing is commonly performed from satellites or aircraft.

Resilience: The ability of a system to recover its capacity to function after disturbance.

Scenario: A coherent description of a potential future situation that serves as input to more detailed analyses or modeling. Scenarios are tools that explore, "if…, then…." statements, and are not predictions of or prescriptions for the future.

Scientific assessments of ozone depletion: Periodic assessments carried out under the auspices of the World Meteorological Organization and the UN Environment Programme of the latest scientific findings related to the ozone layer that fulfill the requirements of an 1987 international agreement known as the "Montreal Protocol on Substances That Deplete the Ozone Layer".

Seasonal timescale: Lasting in the order of roughly 100 days (a season).

Seasonal-to-interannual timescales: Timescales ranging from about 100 days up to a few years. The El Niño-Southern Oscillation (ENSO) is an example of seasonal-to-interannual variability.

Sensitivity: The degree to which a system is affected, either adversely or beneficially, by climate-related stimuli. The effect may be direct (e.g., a change in crop yield in response to a change in the mean, range, or variability of temperature) or indirect (e.g., damages caused by an increase in the frequency of coastal flooding due to sea-level rise).

Sink: Any process, activity, or mechanism that removes a greenhouse gas, an aerosol, or a precursor of a greenhouse gas or aerosol from the atmosphere. Sinks may be of natural or human origin.[64]

Spatial and temporal scales: Climate may vary on a large range of spatial and temporal scales. Spatial scales may range from local (less than 100,000 km^2), through regional (100,000 to 10 million km^2) to continental (10 to 100 million km^2). Temporal scales may range from seasonal to geological (up to hundreds of millions of years).[65]

Stakeholders: Individuals or groups whose interests (financial, cultural, value-based, or other) are affected by climate variability, climate change, or options for adapting to or mitigating these phenomena. Stakeholders are important partners with the research community for development of decision support resources.

Storm surge: The temporary increase, at a particular locality, in the height of the sea due to extreme meteorological conditions (low atmospheric pressure and/or strong winds).[66]

Stressor: A chemical or biological agent, environmental condition, external stimulus or event that stimulates change within an organism or system.

---

64. IPCC, 2007.
65. *Ibid*.
66. *Ibid*.

Subcommittee on Global Change Research (SGCR): The steering committee of the U.S. Global Change Research Program (USGCRP) under the Committee on Environment, Natural Resources, and Sustainability, overseen by the Executive Office of the President. SGCR is composed of representatives from each of the member agencies of the USGCRP.

Sustainability: Balancing the needs of present and future generations while substantially reducing poverty and conserving the planet's life support systems.

Sustainable development: Development which meets the needs of current generations without compromising the ability of future generations to meet their own needs.[67]

Synoptic: Pertaining to motions of whole weather systems, on spatial scales of hundreds to thousands of kilometers and timescales on the order of a few days.[68]

System: Integration of interrelated, interacting, or interdependent components into a complex whole.

Technology: An approach, including both the experimental technique and the instrumental and scientific infrastructure needed to implement it.

Timescale: Characteristic time for a process to be expressed.

Tipping point: A critical threshold at which a tiny perturbation can qualitatively alter the state or development of a system.[69]

Threshold: A point in a system after which any change that is described as *abrupt* is one where the change in the response is much larger than the change in the forcing. The changes at the threshold are therefore abrupt relative to the changes that occur before or after the threshold and can lead to a transition to a new state.[70]

Uncertainty: An expression of the degree to which a value (e.g., the future state of the climate system) is unknown. Uncertainty in future climate arises from imperfect scientific understanding of the behavior of physical systems, and from an inability to predict human behavior.[71]

United Nations Framework Convention on Climate Change: An international treaty produced with the goal of stabilizing atmospheric greenhouse gases at a level that would prevent "dangerous anthropogenic interference with the climate system."

United States Global Change Research Program (USGCRP): An interagency program that coordinates and integrates Federal research on changes in the global environment and their implications for society. USGCRP began as a presidential initiative in 1989 and was mandated by Congress in the Global Change Research Act of 1990 (P.L. 101-606), Thirteen departments and agencies participate in the USGCRP, The program is steered by the Subcommittee on Global Change Research under the Committee on Environment and Natural Resources, overseen by the Executive Office of the President, and facilitated by a National Coordination Office.

---

67. Report of the World Commission on Environment and Development: Our Common Future, 1987 (aka Bruntland Commission).
68. John H. Seinfeld, Spyros N. Pandis. Atmospheric Chemistry and Physics: From Air Pollution to Climate Change. 2nd ed. John Wiley & Sons, Inc. Hoboken, New Jersey. 2006
69. Lenton TM, Held H, Kriegler E, Hall JW, Lucht W, Rahmstorf S, Schellnhuber HJ. Tipping elements in the Earth's Climate System. Proc Natl Acad Sci; 89(2): 13. 2008
70. Seinfeld and Pandis, 2006
71. Lenton et al., 2008

U.S. Group on Earth Observations (USGEO): An interagency group established in 2005 under the White House Office of Science and Technology Policy's Committee on Environment, Natural Resources, and Sustainability to lead Federal efforts to achieve a national Integrated Earth Observation System. Through USGEO, the United States further supports cooperative, international efforts to build the Global Earth Observation System of Systems (GEOSS).

Vienna Convention for the Protection of the Ozone Layer (1985): An international treaty, under the auspices of the United Nations Environment Programme, providing the framework for global efforts to protect the globe's ozone layer.

Vulnerability: The degree to which a system is susceptible to, or unable to cope with, adverse effects of climate and global change, including climate variability and extremes, as well as climate change in conjunction with other stressors.

Weather: The specific condition of the atmosphere at a particular place and time. It is measured in terms of parameters such as wind, temperature, humidity, atmospheric pressure, cloudiness, and precipitation.

Appendix III. Acronym List

ARS: Agricultural Research Service

BIA: Bureau of Indian Affairs

BLM: Bureau of Land Management

CCTP: Climate Change Technology Program

CDC: Centers for Disease Control and Prevention

CENRS: Committee on Environment, Natural Resources, and Sustainability

CEQ: Council on Environmental Quality

DOC: Department of Commerce

DoD: Department of Defense

DOE: Department of Energy

DOI: Department of the Interior

DOT: Department of Transportation

ENSO: El Niño Southern Oscillation

EPA: Environmental Protection Agency

USFWS: United States Fish and Wildlife Service

FY: Fiscal Year (U.S. Federal Government FY is October 1 to September 30)

GEOSS: Global Earth Observation System of Systems

GFCS: Global Framework for Climate Services

HHS: Department of Health and Human Services

IAV: Impacts, Adaptation, and Vulnerability models

ICSU: International Council for Science

IPCC: Intergovernmental Panel on Climate Change

ISSC: International Social Science Council

NASA: National Aeronautics and Space Administration

NCA: National Climate Assessment

NCO: National Coordination Office

NIDIS: National Integrated Drought Information System

NIH: National Institutes of Health

NOAA: National Oceanic and Atmospheric Administration

NPS: National Park Service

NSF: National Science Foundation

NSTC: National Science and Technology Council

OMB: Office of Management and Budget

OSTP: Office of Science and Technology Policy

SGCR: Subcommittee on Global Change Research

SI: Smithsonian Institution

USAID: United States Agency for International Development

USDA: United States Department of Agriculture

USGCRP: United States Global Change Research Program

USGEO: United States Group on Earth Observations

USGS: United States Geological Survey

WCRP: World Climate Research Programme

www.ingramcontent.com/pod-product-compliance
Lightning Source LLC
Chambersburg PA
CBHW080252290526
45790CB00005B/1787